Home for Dinner

A Cookbook for the American Family

By Beverly Black Michels

Cover Painting by Betsy Herrmann

Dedication

Home for Dinner is dedicated to my family. Steve, Bucky, Ted and Maggie; thank you for all your love, support, encouragement and praise. I could not have accomplished this without you.

To all my friends. To Judy and Virginia who encouraged me to start writing this book. To Betsy for believing.

To all you wonderful people who let me cook for you, shared recipes with me and encouraged me to do more. Especially to Mary, a great friend who has kept after me for years to finish this book.

And finally, to every person in America who cooks dinner. May your example encourage many to follow.

Cover Painting

Longtime friend and artist Betsy Herrmann resides with her husband on their farm in northern Maryland. She has two grown daughters. She actively pursues her landscape and animal paintings, produces published graphics and teaches art.

Author's Note

It was 1992 when I decided to write a cookbook. My children were little more than preschoolers. Friends had asked me to teach cooking classes from my home, but I decided I would rather teach through writing. I sat down at my old typewriter from college and began this book.

A lot has changed since then. Today my oldest son is in graduate school. My second son is working on his PhD and my daughter will graduate from college next year. I am now an empty nester who has taken up raising dairy goats and making cheese as a hobby.

We have lived in 3 states, one twice, and I am finishing this book on my third computer.

Our lives have changed and we have grown in so many different ways. One of the few things that have not changed is our desire to get together for a family dinner, whenever possible.

There have been good times, there have been difficult times, but through it all we have managed to come home for dinner.

Bev Michels
February 2008

Table of Contents

Table of Contents Continued

Spring

Spring – my favorite time of the year.
Everything seems to come alive and our senses
are renewed.

The earth smells fresh and green. The sun
radiates warmth and energy. The daffodils and
tulips burst forth with color and beauty.

So too should our food in the spring. Our meals
are best light, full of radiant color with a fresh
new taste.

Spring I

Appetizers

Soups

Salads

Breads

Breakfast Foods

Homemade Boursin Cheese
Serves 6

Homemade Boursin cheese is ever so easy to make and tastes ever so much fresher and better than the expensive store-bought version.

8 ounces cream cheese
4 tablespoons butter, softened
⅓ cup sour cream
½ teaspoon minced garlic
1 heaping teaspoon of chopped fresh parsley*
¼ teaspoon salt
Freshly ground pepper to taste

In a medium mixing bowl beat cream cheese and butter until fluffy. Beat in sour cream, garlic, parsley, salt and pepper. Line a small bowl with plastic wrap and pack Boursin mixture into it. Refrigerate two hours or longer.

Turn out on a board and serve with crackers. Boursin may be made several days in advance. Flavors intensify the longer it is refrigerated.

For a special presentation place an edible flower or a sprig of an herb on the bottom of the plastic wrap *then* pack the Boursin. When you turn out the cheese, the flower will be nicely situated on top.

*For a more herbal cheese add ½ teaspoon chopped fresh marjoram and ½ teaspoon chopped fresh oregano.

Edible Flowers:

Bee balm	**Honeysuckle**	**Tulip**
Calendula	**Common lilac**	**Pansy**
Chamomile	**Marigold**	**Sunflower**
Chrysanthemum	**Nasturtium**	**Daylily**
Dianthus	**Squash blossom**	**Rose**
Scented Geranium	**Rose Mallow**	**Lavender**

Plant an Herb Garden

If planting an herb garden does not change the way you cook, it certainly will enhance it. Herbs are easy to grow and are not picky about their soil. In fact, my best herb gardens have been in towns that have the poorest soil conditions.

They do, however, need sun and water. If outside planting is not possible, place herbs in a small pot on a sunny window soil.

It is amazing how much more you will use herbs in cooking if you have them on hand. Remember to only use the leaves or the flower of the herb, the stems are usually bitter.

Experiment with your herbs. Add them to soups, salads, roasts and grilled foods.

Spring Luncheon

I can think of few better ways to herald the arrival of "good" weather than a casual luncheon on the porch with a few friends who you haven't seen since the holidays.

Set the tone by decorating your porch with little clay pots full of pink geraniums. Scatter the pots around the floor and put one on each table. Also set out a few little bowls full of candy mints in those pretty pastel colors.

That is really all you need, and I guarantee everyone will feel like Spring, even if the weather does not cooperate.

Pineapple Cheese Spread

Carrot Soup

Chicken Salad, garnished with avocado, hard-boiled egg slices and strawberries

Poppyseed Bread and Lemon Bread

Angel Food Cake and Ice Cream

Make the bread a week or two ahead and freeze. Make the cheese spread a day or two in advance. Make the soup a day ahead. Also, boil the eggs a day or two in advance. The cake may be made ahead and frozen or wrapped in foil and refrigerated.

The day of the luncheon all that should need to be made is the chicken salad.

Pineapple Cheese Spread
Serves 6-8

This cheese has the color of Spring and a fresh taste to go along with it. Try serving with ginger snaps or crackers of your choice.

16 ounces cream cheese, softened
One, 8½ ounce can of crushed pineapple, drained
⅓ cup chopped pecans
¼ cup chopped green bell pepper
2 tablespoons chopped scallion tops
1 teaspoon seasoned salt

In a medium mixing bowl place cream cheese, stir in crushed pineapple, pecans, bell pepper, scallions and salt. Cover and chill several hours.

Mixture made be made into a ball and rolled in an additional 1 cup of chopped pecans.

May be made several days in advance and refrigerated.

"If you can't say anything nice, then don't say anything at all."
- Thumper, *Bambi*
This is especially good to remember when you're hosting a dinner party.

Artichokes

Freshly steamed artichokes are great for either an appetizer or a side dish served with baked fish or chicken. My children love them primarily, I think, because they are so much fun to dip and eat.

Allow 1 artichoke per person if used as a vegetable side dish and ½ an artichoke per person if used as an appetizer.

To Clean

Rinse. Pull off lower petals. Cut off the stem so the vegetable will stand upright in a pot. Cut the top part of the artichoke so that it is flat. Trim the sharp points off the outer leaves with scissors.

To Cook

Put enough water in a pan so that when the artichokes are added the depth of the water will be about 3 inches. Add 1 tablespoon lemon juice and ½ teaspoon salt for each 1 quart of water. The lemon juice is necessary to keep the artichokes from turning brown.

Roll the artichokes in the lemon water then stand them upright. Bring the water to a boil. Cover, reduce heat to low and continue to simmer 25 to 40 minutes or until a leaf near the center pulls out easily.

Serve with a dipping sauce of hollandaise, melted butter, mayonnaise, or olive oil with lemon.

To Eat

Artichokes are served whole on a plate, usually with a sauce nearby. Pull out a petal with your fingers, dip the fattest part into the sauce. Then, still holding on, put the petal in your mouth, bite, and pull it through your teeth. When all the leaves are gone, the choke remains. Do not eat this thistle-like portion. Remove choke with a knife to reveal the bottom of the artichoke known as the heart. Cut the heart into bite-sized pieces, dip, and enjoy.

Hollandaise
Makes 1 Cup

This recipe is adapted from Anne Willan. When making hollandaise, it is important to remember to use a heavy pan and low heat so that the egg yolks do not scramble or separate. Don't be upset if the hollandaise doesn't work the first time you try the recipe – try it again. Once you get the knack, it is quite simple and easy to make – and ever so delicious.

¾ cup unsalted butter
2 tablespoons water
3 egg yolks
Juice of ½ a lemon (or to taste)
Salt and pepper to taste

Melt the butter. I prefer to do this in a microwave. Set the melted butter aside.

In a small, heavy saucepan, whisk together the water and egg yolks until thoroughly combined and light in color-about 30 seconds.

Place saucepan over low-medium heat, whisking eggs constantly. Begin pouring butter drop by drop into eggs. Continue to whisk and pour butter by drops until all in incorporated into the sauce. (Leave the milky whey in the bottom of the butter dish.)

Remove from heat and stir in lemon juice. Add salt and pepper to taste. Serve.

Hollandaise begins to thicken as it cools. Unfortunately, I have never been able to find a way to reheat the sauce without having it separate

Enjoy this wonderful sauce when it is made. It is fantastic on most vegetables and always a welcome addition to broiled or poached fish

Artichokes Stuffed with Goat Cheese and Herbs
Serves 4 as a first course or side dish
Serves 8-10 as an appetizer

4 medium artichokes, tops and stems trimmed
Juice of ½ a lemon

1 tablespoon chopped fresh parsley leaves
1 tablespoon chopped fresh chives
1½ teaspoons chopped fresh tarragon leaves
1 medium scallion, cleaned, diced
8 ounces cream cheese
¼ pound goat cheese
¼ cup whipping cream or milk
Salt and pepper to taste

In a large, flat bottomed saucepan, add water about 3 inches deep, and lemon juice. Stand artichokes upright in saucepan and bring water to a boil. When water boils, cover and reduce heat to low. Simmer artichokes for approximately 35 minutes or until done.

While the artichokes are cooking, prepare the goat cheese mixture. In a food processor or mixer combine cream cheese, goat cheese, and whipping cream. Process or beat until mixture is smooth. Add salt and pepper to taste.

Add herbs and scallion to cheese mixture. Process until smooth. Adjust seasonings to taste.

The cheese mixture may be prepared several days in advance. Wrap in plastic wrap and keep refrigerated.

When the artichokes are done cooking, remove them from the water and drain. Cool. Carefully remove the tiny, paper-thin, center leaves. With a spoon scoop out the choke, being careful to keep the artichoke intact.

Spoon 2 to 3 tablespoons of cheese mixture into the center of each artichoke. Place each artichoke on a piece of aluminum foil large enough to cover the artichoke completely.

Gather foil up around the artichoke, twisting at top to secure. (Can be prepared one day ahead of time and refrigerated.)

In a preheated, 350 degree oven, place artichokes on a baking sheet until heated through. About 10-15 minutes, depending on whether or not the artichokes had been refrigerated.

Unwrap the artichoke. Place each on the center of a plate. To eat, dip leaves in the cheese mixture as you would a sauce.

Any cheese mixture that is not used to stuff the artichokes is delicious refrigerated then served on crackers as an appetizer.

Did you know that goat cheese has lower calories, saturated fat and cholesterol than most other cheeses? One ounce of goat cheese has 70 calories, 4 grams saturated fat and 15 milligrams of cholesterol. While 1 ounce of cheddar cheese has 110 calories, 6 grams of saturated fat and 40 milligrams of cholesterol. And 1 ounce of Parmigiano Reggiano contains 115 calories, 5.5 grams of saturated fat and 17 milligrams of cholesterol.*

*Grassi Parmigiano Reggiano, Tillamook Sharp Cheddar Cheese, and Trader Joe's Chevre were used for these statistics.

Parmesan Cheese Sticks
Serves 6-8
Probably one of my oldest and most requested recipes.

10 slices of coarse white bread, such as English muffin loaf
3 cups freshly grated Parmesan cheese
1 cup butter (2 sticks), melted

Preheat oven to 400 degrees.

Remove crust from bread and discard. Cut the bread in to 1 inch strips. Individually dip the strips into butter and place on wax paper. Pile about a tablespoon of cheese onto each strip. Place on cookie sheet.*

Bake 8-10 minutes or until slightly browned. Serve warm.

* Cheese sticks may be frozen at this stage then repackaged for long-term freezing. Frozen cheese sticks may be placed directly into a hot oven. Cooking time will be slightly longer.

$\frac{1}{3}$

The Neighbors for Dinner
An Italian Dinner for 12

What better way to get to know your new neighbors than to invite them to a dinner along with a couple of friends up, down, and around the block.

Neighborhood parties are best kept casual and relaxed, especially when this is the first meeting for many.

To help create an Italian theme, use plaid tablecloths and empty wine bottles as candle holders. For place cards, I had my then 7-year-old son draw the Italian flag with each guest's name on plain white cars we had made from construction paper.

Italian Cheese and Crackers
Memorable Mussels

Minestrone
Crusty Bread

Cheese Stuffed Shells with Tomato and Sausage Sauce
Tossed Salad

Chocolate Torte
Cheesecake with Fresh Berries

Make pasta shells and sauce several weeks in advance and freeze, if desired.

The cheesecake can be made 3 or 4 days in advance. The chocolate torte can be made the day ahead. The soup may also be made one day in advance.

The day of the party, all that needs to be done is to assemble the cheese tray, make the mussels and prepare the salad. This should leave plenty of time for you to relax and make sure you and your company are enjoying yourselves.

Memorable Mussels
Serves 6-8

This appetizer makes an impressive presentation before a dinner party. Place the mussels in a large attractive bowl and ladle into a small soup bowls to serve. If guests are serving themselves, be sure to tell them to place extra sauce over their mussels.

To serve as a main dish, remove mussels from shell and toss with the cooking sauce over pasta. This recipe is adapted from Jane Broody's <u>Good Food Gourmet.</u>

5 pounds mussels, scrubbed and debearded
½ cup chopped scallions
1 tablespoon olive oil
¼ cup chopped fresh parsley leaves
3 tablespoons chopped fresh basil, or 1½ tablespoon dried
1 tablespoon finely minced garlic (about 3 cloves)
½ teaspoon crushed red pepper, or to taste
¾ dry white wine
Fresh ground pepper to taste

Place the mussels in a large pot. Add remaining ingredients and cover. Bring the liquid to a boil and cook the mussels over high heat for 5-8 minutes or until the mussels open.

According to <u>Larousse Gastronomique,</u> mussels bought live must be firmly closed and cooked within three days of being caught. (Mussels which do not close when they are tapped must be thrown away.) Mussels are high in calcium, iron, and iodine. They are nicknamed 'the poor man's oyster' because of their abundance and reasonable price.

Minestrone
Serves 10-12

There are hundreds if not thousands of recipes for minestrone, the well known Italian soup. In an effort to determine what makes a minestrone a minestrone, I found that the key ingredients are pasta, beans, and an assortment of vegetables with zucchini ever-present.

The soup can be made with a beef or chicken stock. It can also be made with a wide assortment of meats and just about any vegetable.

So be adventurous and make your own famous family minestrone recipe by simply varying a few ingredients.

This recipe is light, with no meat, and is particularly good as a first course before a pasta dinner. It is equally good for lunch with a crusty loaf of bread or sandwiches.

2 tablespoons of olive oil
2 carrots, peeled and diced
1 medium onion, diced
10 cups chicken stock (2½ quarts)
2 leeks, white part only, rinsed and finely chopped
1 garlic clove, crushed
1 bay leaf
2 cups canned white beans, drained*
Salt and pepper to taste
3 ounces small pasta, such as bow ties
3 or 4 canned tomatoes (about ½ of a 15 ounce-can),
    drained and chopped
2 small zucchinis, cut in ¼ inch slices
2 tablespoons chopped fresh parsley
freshly grated Parmesan cheese

In a large 5-6 quart pot, heat the oil. Add the carrots and onions and sauté until soft. Add the stock, leeks, garlic, bay leaf and beans. Season with salt and pepper. Bring to a boil. Reduce heat to a simmer and cook about 30 minutes.

Add pasta tomatoes, zucchini, and parsley. Simmer for an additional 10-15 minutes.

Serve with freshly grated Parmesan cheese.

May be frozen.

*2/3 cup raw navy beans may be substituted for canned beans. Soak raw beans overnight. Then simmer in water for about 2 hours or until tender. Beans are then ready to add to soup.

"Probably the most satisfying soup in the world for people who are hungry, as well as for those who are tired or worried or cross or in debt or in a moderate amount of pain or in love or in robust health or in any kind of business hugger muggery, is minestrone."
-    **M. F. K. Fisher, The Art of Eating**

Soup: n. A liquid made by boiling meats, fish or vegetables with various added ingredients.
- The Random House Dictionary

Carrot Soup
Serves 4-6

This is a light soup with beautiful color and great flavor. It may be served hot or cold. This recipe is adapted from The Silver Palate Cookbook by Julee Rosso and Sheila Lukins.

4 tablespoons butter
1 cup chopped leeks, white part only
1 cup chopped onion
1½ pound carrots, cleaned and roughly chopped
4 cups chicken stock
1 cup orange juice

In a stockpot melt the butter. Add leeks and onions and sauté until soft. Add carrots and chicken stock. Bring to a boil. Reduce heat to a simmer and continue to cook on low until carrots are soft. About 30 minutes.

Run mixture through a food mill or puree in a blender. Return to pot. Stir in orange juice. If a thinner consistency is desired, add more chicken stock. Add salt and pepper to taste.

Serve hot or cold.

How many carrots does one need to eat to obtain bright eyes?

Easter Dinner

Easter dinners should be as colorful and festive as the eggs that were hunted earlier in the day. The dinner should rival the finest of bonnets and compliment every lady's Spring attire.

As with any other holiday celebration, keep the meal easy to prepare and with much of the work done ahead of time.

Homemade Boursin Cheese with edible flowers, assorted crackers and fruit (such as strawberries and grapes)

Asparagus Soup

Butterflied Leg of Lamb
Oven Roasted Potatoes
Steamed Sugar Peas

Cheesecake with Chocolate shavings

The boursin may be prepared several days in advance. The soup may also be prepared a day ahead. The lamb should be put in the marinade 24 hours in advance. And, the cheesecake can be made up to 3 days before the dinner. The potatoes may be roasted earlier in the day and served at room temperature.

When guests and family arrive all that should be left to do is grill or roast the lamb and steam the peas.

Easter Egg Dye

Dying Easter eggs is actually a cooking procedure. It is also a good chemistry lesson for your youngsters. But most importantly: it is more fun to create your own dye and your own colors. The number of colors you care to create are limited only by your imagination and the color wheel.

Boil eggs in an enamel, stainless steel or glass container. Do not use aluminum or iron.

For each color, place 1 tablespoon white vinegar with ½ cup cold water in a small bowl. Add 5-6 drops of food color. Turn hard boiled egg several times in color to coat evenly. The longer the egg is left in the color, the darker it will become.

To decorate eggs, use a wax crayon to write or draw on the egg before dying it.

Asparagus Soup
Serves 4-6

2 tablespoons olive oil
1 tablespoon butter
1 small/medium onion, peeled and sliced
1 pound fresh green asparagus
4 tablespoons flour
6 cups water
2 teaspoons salt

In a quart (or larger) pan, melt butter and olive oil. Add sliced onion and sauté over medium-low heat until soft.

Clean asparagus. Trim away tough bottoms. Cut the tender tops into 3 inch spears and set aside. Cut the stems in to ¾ inch pieces.

In a large pot place 6 cups of water and salt. Bring to a boil. Add asparagus stems and boil, uncovered, for 5 minutes. Remove asparagus with slotted spoon and set aside.

Bring water back to a boil and add asparagus tops. Boil, uncovered, for 6-8 minutes or until just tender. With a slotted spoon remove tops and set aside. Reserve water.

Add asparagus stems to cooked onions. Cover and cook slowly on low heat for 5 minutes. Stir in flour and continue to cook and stir for several minutes.

Remove from hear and stir in ½ cup of reserved water; gradually adding the rest. Return to heat and simmer slowly, partially covered, for about 25 minutes or until stalks are very tender.

Line up blanched asparagus tops. Cut off ¼ inch top. Reserve for garnish.

Puree the rest of the asparagus tops with the soup. The soup can be made ahead up to this point. Soup can also be frozen at this point.

Return soup to pan and heat. Thin with milk if a thinner consistency if desired.

Serve in bowls garnished with reserved tips. Soup may be served hot or cold.

The technique for this recipe is adapted from Mastering the Art of French Cooking by Julia Child, Volume Two.

"He that scatters thorns, let him not go barefoot."
- Benjamin Franklin

Celebrate!

Cooking and special meals are the means by which we mark and celebrate our lives.

To me, every day should be a celebration of living, a toast to life, a toast to food, a toast to love, a toast to friends and family.

Don't wait for a birthday to make your child's favorite cake. Don't wait for Thanksgiving to cook a turkey. Today is a good day to celebrate. Celebrate it by making a favorite meal.

"It doesn't have to be a major event to cook lunch or dinner."
-Emeril Lagasse

Poppy Seed Salad Dressing
About 1 Pint

Poppy seed dressing is at its best when drizzled over fresh fruit that has been mounded on a few leaves of lettuce. Strawberries, blueberries, and melons are all excellent fruits to use with poppy seed dressing. This recipe is adapted from my friend, Debbie Vaky.

¾ cup sugar
1 teaspoon dry mustard
⅓ cup red wine vinegar
1 tablespoon onion juice (available in the spice section of most groceries)
1 cup vegetable oil or canola oil
1 tablespoon poppy seeds
Dash of salt

In a blender or food processor, place sugar, dry mustard, vinegar, and onion juice. Blend. With the blender running, slowly add oil until all is incorporated. Stir in poppy seeds and salt.

May be kept refrigerated for several weeks.

Mother's Day
Send Mom Breakfast in Bed

Perhaps my fondest memories of Mother's Day are the ones when I awoke to wide-eyed toddlers in over-sized pajamas with a carefully held tray of coffee, juice, and toast. The smiles on their faces and the twinkle in their eyes filled the bedroom with so much sunshine, that I don't remember a cloudy Mother's Day.

This year, try sending your mom breakfast in bed. She'll probably enjoy it much more than a fancy, store-bought gift.

Four days before Mother's Day, have your children make a card for their Grandmothers. I usually have them draw a bouquet of flowers. Then I cut out the heads of old family pictures or left-over school pictures and place them in the center of the flowers. Voila! A Mother's Day card from the bunch!

Next, go out and purchase a small amount of specialty coffee or tea and grocery shop for the bread you will make.

Three days before Mother's Day, get up and make some bread. I like sending the small loaves, usually two different kinds. My favorite combination is poppy seed bread and strawberry bread.

Bread recipes made with oil tend to stay fresh longer, so those are the ones I usually chose.

While the bread is cooling, find an old shoebox, fill it with some pretty tissue paper. Then wrap your bread in plastic wrap, tie it with a bow and place it in the box with the coffee and card. Then off to the post office.

Take the next two days to relax and then enjoy your own Mother's Day.

The U.S. Post Office claims that any package mailed first class to anywhere within the continental U.S. will reach its destination within three days.

Strawberry Bread
2 loaves

This recipe may be made with fresh or frozen strawberries with equally good results.

1 quart fresh strawberries, cleaned and sliced OR 1 pound packaged frozen strawberries, thawed, drained.
1 cup pecans, pulverized
3 cups flour
2 cups sugar
1 teaspoon cinnamon
1 teaspoon baking soda
1 teaspoon salt
4 eggs well beaten
1¼ cups vegetable oil

Grease two 4½ X 8½ inch loaf pans. Preheat oven to 350 degrees. Process pecans in a blender of food processor until pulverized. In a large mixing bowl place pecans, flour, sugar, cinnamon, baking soda, and salt. Stir to mix.

Make a well in the center of the flour mixture and pour in eggs, oil and strawberries. Stir until well blended. Divide the batter between the two baking pans. Bake approximately 1 hour or until done. Bread is done when a cake tester inserted into the center of the loaf comes out clean. Cool on rack.

Strawberry Spread

To make a tasty spread for your strawberry bread, combine one 8-ounce package of cream cheese with ¼ cup strawberry jam. Beat together until mixed.

Make smaller loaves or muffins with most sweet bread recipes. Simply adjust baking times accordingly.

To Grease or Not To Grease

There are many different methods to prepare a pan for baking. One may use butter, margarine, vegetable oil, or a cooking spray. All work fine. In this cookbook, the term to "grease" is used as the technique to prepare a pan for baking. This allows the individual to choose whether they prefer to use butter, oil, or a cooking spray.

Poppy Seed Bread with Orange Glaze

1 large loaf

3 cups flour
1½ teaspoon baking powder
1½ teaspoon salt
2½ cups sugar
3 eggs
1 cup plus 2 tablespoons vegetable oil
1½ cups milk
1½ teaspoons vanilla
1 teaspoon almond extract
2 tablespoons poppy seeds

For the glaze: ½ cup sugar plus 2 tablespoons orange juice mixed together.

Grease and flour a 9 x 5 inch loaf pan. Preheat oven to 350 degrees. In a large mixing bowl sift together the flour, baking powder and salt. Stir in sugar. Make a well in the center and pour in eggs, oil, and milk. Stir until well blended. Stir in vanilla, almond extract, and poppy seeds.

Pour batter into loaf pan. Bake 1-1½ hours or until done. Bread is done when a cake tester is inserted into the center of the bread and comes out clean.

Place bread on rack and pour orange glaze over. Let cool completely before slicing.

Lemon Bread
1 large loaf

Excellent with chicken salad, or try the bread sliced and toasted with butter for breakfast.

1 cup butter (2 sticks)
1 cup sugar
4 eggs
¼ cup lemon juice
¼ cup buttermilk
2 teaspoons freshly grated lemon peel
2 cups flour
2 teaspoons baking powder
1 teaspoon salt

Butter a 9 x 5 inch loaf pan. Preheat oven to 375 degrees. In a medium mixing bowl, cream together butter and sugar until light and fluffy. Beat in eggs one at a time. Stir in lemon juice, buttermilk, and lemon peel.

In a separate bowl, sift together flour, baking powder, and salt. Stir flour mixture into eggs, butter and sugar mixture. Pour into loaf pan. Bake 50-60 minutes or until done. Bread is done when a cake tester inserted into center of loaf comes out clean. Cool on rack. Freezes well.

Spring Brunch

A light brunch on a Spring Sunday morning is a delightful way to entertain a few friends or an even better way to turn an average Sunday into a special family occasion.

Two Cheese Quiche
Steamed Asparagus
Fruit Salad with Poppy Seed Dressing

Lemon Coconut and Chocolate Tart

Dining partners, regardless of gender, social standing, or the years they've lived, should be chosen for their ability to eat- and drink! – with the right mixture of abandon and restraint. They should enjoy food, and look upon its preparation and its degutation as one of the human arts.
They should relish the accompanying drinks, whether they be ale from a bottle on a hillside or the ripe bouquet of a Chanbertin 1919 in a great crystal globe on the finest damask.
And, above all, friends should possess the rare gift of sitting. They should be able, no, eager, to sit for hours-three, four, six- over a meal of soup and wine and cheese, as well as one of twenty fabulous courses.
Then , with good friends of such attributes, and good food on the board, and good wine in the pitcher, we may well ask, when shall we live if not now?
- <u>The Art of Eating</u> *by M.F.K. Fisher.*

Two Cheese Quiche
Serves 4-6

Quiche is making a welcome comeback. It is a great dish for brunch, lunch, or a light dinner. It is easily varied by adding cooked spinach, crumbled crisp bacon, mushrooms, cooked chicken or ham, asparagus, seafood, or just about anything you're in the mood to eat!

The two cheeses give this quiche an interesting flavor, although one cheese may be substituted and any of the above ingredients may be added.

Pastry for one 9-inch pie shell
4 ounces shredded Swiss or Gruyere cheese
4 ounces shredded Cheddar cheese
1 tablespoon minced shallots
1 tablespoon butter
3 eggs
1½ cups milk
½ teaspoon salt
Dash nutmeg
Freshly ground pepper to taste

Preheat oven to 450 degrees. Shred cheeses, set aside. In a small skillet, melt the butter and sauté the shallots until soft.

Line a 9-inch pie pan or quiche pan with pastry. Scatter shallots over bottom. Top with cheeses.

In a medium mixing bowl, whisk together eggs, milk, salt, nutmeg, and pepper. Pour egg mixture over cheeses.

Place in preheated oven and bake 15 minutes. Reduce heat to 325 degrees and continue to bake for an additional 30 minutes or until quiche is set. Remove from oven and let cool slightly on rack before slicing.

Serve warm, room temperature, or cold.

Spring II

Entrees

Side Dishes

Baseball Season

When my six-year-old started playing baseball, I was amazed when the coach said there would be practice once or twice a week and two games a week. When or how was I going to fix dinner – let alone eat it? The coach did not have an answer and the first season was painful and exhausting.

But my six-year-old loved baseball, and my 5-year-old, 2-year-old, and I learned to survive. Fix dinners in the morning or afternoon or whenever there are a few free minutes (and I know there are only a rare few minutes of free time.)

A favorite do-ahead is grilled hamburgers. Start the grill when you have lunch, when the kids come home, or while you're waiting for someone to get their uniform. Grill your burgers, put them on a roll and wrap them up in a paper towel and refrigerate. When it's time to eat – zap them in the microwave. Few people will know they didn't just come off the grill.

Make your taco mixture up at breakfast. Refrigerate. Slice the lettuce and tomatoes and grate the cheese later in the day while your child finds his water bottle and puts on his cleats. Dinner will take minutes to put on the table and will taste delicious when you get home.

Roast a whole chicken during the day. Chicken is often the best when served at room temperature. Dinners don't have to all be hot. Room temperature and even cold works well for chicken and ham.

Stay away from the fast-food trap. Sure it may be easier to stop at the local fast-food establishment on the way to the game for the pre-schooler and again on the way home for the baseball player – but it just is not that good for you, the kids, or the family.

A little planning ahead can go a long way to providing a nutritional, home-made meal when there is no time to cook.

"It's natural for us to be overweight because our culture is sedentary and eats big portions. That's not mysterious; it's inevitable. You don't need to invoke molecular biology when the problem is fast-food restaurants."
- **Dr. John Foreyt, a leading obesity researcher**

Lavender Scented Chicken
Serves 4

This chicken dish not only tastes delicious, but it has the added beauty of perfuming your home with the sweet scent of lavender. It is a "must try" poultry dish.

2 teaspoons dried, untreated, lavender flowers,
    available in the spice section of many food stores
6 tablespoons butter, softened
1 teaspoon minced fresh thyme leaves
½ teaspoon finely grated fresh lemon zest
1 3-4 pound chicken
1 small lemon halved

In a small bowl, combine the lavender, butter, thyme, and lemon zest. Spoon mixture on a sheet of plastic wrap or wax paper and form into a log. Chill butter mixture until firm, at least 30 minutes and up to 3 days.

Preheat over to 425 degrees. Rinse the bird inside and out and pat dry. Season inside cavity with salt and pepper. Starting at the neck end of the bird, slide fingers between meat and skin to loosen skin (be careful not to tear). Cut butter into ¼ inch thick slices. Gently push slices under skin of bird, reserving about 4 slices. Ties legs of the bird together with kitchen string and secure wings to sides.

Place chicken in roasting pan. Squeeze lemon juice over. Season with salt and pepper. Place reserved butter slices on top of breast and thighs.

Roast chicken for 15 minutes then reduce heat to 350 degrees. Baste bird with pan drippings and continue to baste every 20 minutes until bird is done – when the meat thermometer registers 175-180 degrees – approximately 45 additional minutes. Total cooking time should be about 1 hour. Remove bird from pan. Tent with foil, and let rest 15 minutes before carving.

If sauce is desired, skim fat from pan drippings. Place pan with drippings over medium heat and bring to a boil. Several tablespoons of white wine may be added at this point. Continue to boil until mixture has reduced by half. Spoon over chicken when it is served.

Garnish with additional lavender flowers if desired.

This dish may be complimented by roasting small onions, carrots and cut-up potatoes along with the chicken. Add vegetables to roasting pan when heat is reduced to 350 degrees. Vegetables should be done at the same time as chicken.

Kitchen String: Yes, you can buy kitchen string, but there are wonderful substitutes. Dental floss works perfectly, although I don't recommend using the flavored variety. My all time favorite kitchen string, however, is kite string. There always seems to be an abundance of it in the basement or the garage and it comes on the nice big spools. I have also resorted to garden string at times, but that can be too thick and heavy. I almost used a clothesline once, but fortunately, the kids found more kite string first! So please don't make a special trip to the store for kitchen string; use what's on hand.

Chicken Salad
Serves 4

This basic chicken salad recipe is easily dressed-up and changed to suit any occasion or taste.

4 boneless, skinless chicken breast-halves (about 1¼ lbs.)
½ cup cleaned and chopped celery
½ cup mayonnaise
1 teaspoon fresh lemon juice
Salt and pepper to taste

In a medium pot, place chicken, cover with water and add 1 teaspoon salt. Bring to a boil. Reduce heat to a simmer and continue to cook for 10 minutes. Remove from heat. Let chicken cool in cooking water – about 30 minutes.

Shred chicken into a mixing bowl. Stir in celery, mayonnaise, and lemon juice. Add salt and pepper to taste.

Refrigerate until cooled.

For variations add: sliced water chestnuts and grapes, a tablespoon or two of your favorite chutney, or chopped pineapple and toasted pecans.

Serve on a bed of lettuce, in a tomato, alongside fresh melon or garnished with strawberries and mango.

Never talk with food in your mouth.

Split Cornish Game Hens with Herbs and White Wine
Serves 4

2 Cornish Game Hens, split in half lengthwise
2 tablespoons olive oil
1 cup dry white wine
1 tablespoon chopped fresh parsley
1 teaspoon chopped fresh rosemary
½ teaspoon chopped garlic
1 bay leaf
4-5 fresh basil leaves, or 1 teaspoon Italian seasoning
2 cloves
¼ cup freshly grated Parmesan cheese

In a large skillet (12 inches) heat olive oil. Salt and pepper birds. Place Cornish Game Hens in skillet, working in batches if necessary. Brown on both sides. Remove birds to a platter.

Pour out any excess oil. Add remaining ingredients, except cheese, to skillet. Bring mixture to a boil. Reduce heat to a simmer. Return birds to skillet. Cover pan and continue to simmer. Turn birds occasionally as they cook until meat is very tender and almost comes off bone, about 30-40 minutes. (Hens may be made ahead up to this point. They may be covered and refrigerated up to 24 hours in advance.)

Heat over to 450 degrees. Place cooked hens in a shallow baking dish. Remove fat from liquid. Pour remaining cooking juices over birds. Pat Parmesan cheese on the hens. Place in top third of oven and bake 10 minutes, on until cheese melts and forms a brown crust.

"There are no guarantees in life."
-Pastor John E. Corson, San Ramon United Methodist Church, April 1997.

Always and Sometimes

Always use Unsalted Butter: It is sweeter and if you want more salt, add it.

Always use All Purpose Unbleached Flour, unless a specific flour is called for.

Always Measure Flour by Leveling the Measuring Cup With A Knife. Never pound or pack flour into measuring cup.

Always Try and Plan Meals Around Seasonal Fruits and Vegetables.

Always Try to Compost.

Always Try to Purchase Fruits and Vegetables Grown in the United States. The closer the food is grown to your home, the fresher and better it will taste.

Always Read Through a Recipe Before Beginning to Cook.

Always Try to Enjoy Life.

Sometimes Try to Make Your Own Chicken Stock

Sometimes Try to Make Your Own Salad Dressing.

Sometimes Try a New Recipe.

Sometimes Cook Dinner for a Friend.

Sometimes Make a Romantic Dinner for Your Significant Other.

Grilled Rainbow Trout

When trout season opens, the kids, the dogs and I usually can be found with our can of corn and maybe some worms, down at the river looking for the illusive fish.

Usually, I end up going to the grocery later that afternoon buying a trout that looks like the one that got away.

As in picking out any fish, always look for clear bright eyes and no smell. Fish shouldn't smell and any reputable fish monger should be glad to let you see for yourself. If he doesn't, go buy your fish elsewhere.

I love to cook my trout whole, but if the head bothers you, have the fish monger cut it off.

This recipe is adapted form <u>James Beard's New Fish Cookery</u> and it is the best I have ever found.

Allow one trout per person.

Rinse and pat dry the trout. Season the inside with salt and pepper. Dip each fish in flour, inside and out. Then dip in a mixture of equal amounts olive oil and melted butter.

Place fish over hot coals and cook, turning once until the meat flakes. About 5-7 minutes per side. Serve with fresh lemon slices.

To eat the trout, peel back the skin and remove the fillet. Then, beginning at the head, lift the skeleton out. Remove the remaining fillet. The host may fillet each fish, or I like to serve each guest a whole fish, placing a platter on the table on which to put the skin and bones.

Always find one thing on which to compliment the host while you are enjoying his or her company. This is a good suggestion even if you are not enjoying the company.

Grilled Pork with Mustard Sauce accented by Carrots and Asparagus

Serves 4

1½ pound pork tenderloin or loin roast
¾ cup olive oil
¼ cup dry white wine
3 cloves garlic, crushed

For the Mustard Sauce
¾ cup dry white wine
1 tablespoon minced shallot
1 cup cream
3 tablespoons Dijon Mustard

3 large carrots
1 pound asparagus

In a small dish just large enough to hold pork, combine oil, wine, and garlic. Add pork, cover and refrigerate overnight. Or pork may be marinated at room temperature or 30-60 minutes before cooking.

Drain pork and discard marinade. Grill on oiled rack approximately 6 inches from glowing coals. Cook about 20 minutes, turning occasionally. A meat thermometer should register 160 degrees when inserted in the center of the loin. Cover and let meat rest several minutes before slicing. Slice 1 inch thick.

To make the Sauce:

In a heavy sauce pan, boil the wine and shallot until reduced to 3 tablespoons of liquid. Strain. Return liquid to pan. Add the cream and bring to a boil, simmer 2 minutes or until just slightly thickened. Remove from heat. Whisk in mustard. Add salt and pepper to taste.

To make carrots and asparagus:

Scrape carrots. Cut in half then slice pencil thin. Wash and trim asparagus. In a large, flat pan that will hold asparagus and carrots, place several inches of water. Add 1 teaspoon salt and a generous squeeze of lemon. Bring to a boil. Add carrots and asparagus and simmer until tender, about 10 minutes.

Presentation:

Puddle several tablespoons of sauce on each serving plate. Arrange several spears of asparagus lengthwise on the bottom of the plate. Place the meat on the sauce, in the center of the plate (above the asparagus). Arrange carrots in a spike-like fashion above the meat.

One of my children once commented that this dinner looks like the sun setting behind the mountains.

Spring Dinner for House Guests

When entertaining house guests no one want to spend the day in the kitchen. However, it is very nice to provide a lovely dinner for your guests. The secret is to plan a menu with recipes that may either be frozen or made ahead of time.

This menu incorporates a frozen appetizer and a dessert that may be made the day before guests arrive.

Sun dried Tomato Canapés

Slow Roasted Sesame Pork with Plum Sauce
Risotto with Herbs de Provence
Steamed Green Beans
Crusty Bread

Meringue Cake with Lemon Cream and Strawberry Sauce

Slow Roasted Sesame Pork with Plum Sauce
Serves 6

This is an elegant meal to serve to guests, yet simple enough to serve to the family on a regular basis. I think the secret to cooking good pork or ham is to use a low heat so the meat stays moist and tasty.

The pork is delicious by itself, but extra good when served with plum sauce.

1 3-pound pork loin or tenderloin
¼ cup honey
¼ soy sauce
½ cup chicken stock
1 tablespoon sesame seeds
salt and pepper

Plum Sauce
¾ cup plum preserves
¾ cup chicken broth
2 tablespoons butter
¼ cup sherry
1½ teaspoons lemon juice
1 teaspoon cornstarch
1 tablespoon water

To marinate the pork: combine the honey, soy sauce, chicken stock, and sesame seeds. Place sauce in roasting pan. Salt and pepper pork. Place pork in the roasting pan with the marinade. Let stand at room temperature for several hours, turning occasionally, or cover and refrigerate over night.

Preheat over to 300 degrees. Bake pork and marinade in roasting pan for approximately 1 hour and 45 minutes, about 35 minutes per pound, or until meat thermometer registers 160 degrees. Baste occasionally with marinade during roasting. If necessary, add water to maintain liquid in roasting pan. When pork is done, remove it from the oven. Cover with foil and let stand 15 minutes before carving. Serve with plum sauce, if desired.

To make the plum sauce

In a small saucepan combine plum preserves, chicken broth, butter, sherry, and lemon juice. Bring to a boil. Reduce heat to a simmer and simmer the sauce for 30 minutes. To thicken, mix cornstarch with water and add to sauce. Continue to stir and cook until sauce thickens. Sauce may be made a day ahead and reheated.

"Balance the day, not each meal in the day."
- M.F.K. Fisher, <u>The Art of Eating</u>

Risotto with Herbs de Provence
Serves 6

Although a little more work-intensive than steamed rice, risotto has become a favorite food with pork or chicken in our house. The creamy texture is especially soothing in the cooler months.

3 tablespoons olive oil
1 tablespoon minced shallots (about 2 shallots)
1½ cup Arborio rice
2½ cups chicken stock
½ cup dry white wine
1 tablespoon Herbs de Provence
freshly grated Parmesan cheese (optional)

In a heavy saucepan, heat olive oil over medium heat. Add shallots and sauté until they are soft. Do not brown. Add the rice and stir well. Continue to cook and stir over medium heat until rice is opaque.

In a large measuring cup or pitcher with a spout, combine stock, wine and herbs. Pour ½ cup of mixture into rice and stir and cook over medium heat until all the liquid has been absorbed. Add another ½ cup of liquid and repeat until all the liquid is used. Stir constantly to keep rice from sticking to bottom. The whole process should take 20-25 minutes.

Parmesan cheese may be sprinkled on rice, or passed on the side if desired.

"I watched how Mother got satisfaction from cooking and making others happy. It took me a little while to understand this was a mission in my life too."
- Paul Prudhomme

Thoughts on Life

It took me ten years to stop feeling guilty about being a stay-at-home mom. I think back on the hours I spent worrying that I should be working and earning money, and I now realize that what I was doing was worth more than money.

Nurturing three children, giving them love, and trying to teach them values and set a good example, changing diapers, and driving carpools- now that is more than a job!

In addition I had a husband whom I loved and for whom I tried to make life happier and nicer.

It was a life without frills: no fancy vacations, no expensive cars. However, I have now come to realize that no amount of money can compare to the rewards of giving the best years of your life to your children and your spouse.

Sitting down to dinner, I often look around in amazement and realize that these wonderful, happy, and healthy people are in part the product of a dedicated mother, and I am fortunate enough to be that woman.

Turn It Green!! St. Patrick's Day Dinner

St. Patrick's Day is a good day to celebrate with food whether you're Irish or not!

Buy a bottle of green food color and you're ready for a fun family evening.

The children will be hysterical when they sit down to dinner and find green milk. They will marvel at the green pears and green cottage cheese. And green pie for dessert? Why not???

The traditional St. Patrick's Day meal is a boiled dinner of corned beef, cabbage, potatoes, and green beans. The meal is easy to prepare, always delicious, and clean-up is a one-pot shot.

One large pot that will hold the corned beef, potatoes, cabbage, and green beans.

Corned Beef:
Allow ½ pound per person. Remove beef from package and rinse. Place beef in pot and add water (enough so that meat and all vegetables will be covered when they are added). Add 1-2 heaping teaspoons of salt. For cooking time allow 1 hour per pound. Bring water to a boil. Reduce heat to a low simmer. The secret to good corned beef is to simmer, **not boil,** on a very low heat. To serve, always slice beef very thin and cut across the grain.

Red Potatoes:
Cut in half, or quartered if very large. Simmer with corned beef for 1 hour. Allow 1 medium potato per person.

Cabbage:
Cut into quarters and remove core. Simmer with beef for 30 minutes. One medium cabbage provides about 4 servings.

Frozen Green Beans:
Simmer with beef for 10 minutes. Allow one handful of beans per serving.

Green Pear and Cottage Cheese:
Place several drops of green food color in a can of pears. Stir and let sit several minutes so that the color can absorb into the fruit. Add several drops of green to a container of cottage cheese, stir. Drain the liquid from the pears. For each serving, line a plate with lettuce, top with a spoonful of cottage cheese and a slice or two of pear.

Kiwi Pie

Accompaniments:
Mustard and/or horseradish for the beef.
Cider vinegar for the cabbage.
Green beverages, such as milk, beer, water, or whatever.

It's Almost Summer Dinner

It seems spring just begins and then it feels like summer. And as soon as it feels like summer it is time to crank-up the grill. A grilled steak is still one of my all-time favorites. Try the left-overs for lunch the next day sliced up in a salad and sprinkled with blue cheese.

The tastes of spring warm into the tastes of summer with this easy to prepare dinner. And what better way to end the season opener of the grill than with roasted marshmallows?

Artichokes with Hollandaise Sauce

Marinated Grilled Steak
Two Bean Salad
Steamed Green Beans
Crusty Bread

Roasted Marshmallows and/or S'mores – To make S'mores place a roasted marshmallow between two graham crackers with a piece of chocolate.

Marinated Grilled Steak
Serves 6

As my boys grew into teenagers, they somehow, somewhere, developed a taste for steak. (It must be a male thing.) However, feeding two bottomless pits filet mignon was not in our budget. Then I found this marinade recipe my mother had given me years ago. Bingo! An inexpensive sirloin tastes as good, or better, as some of the finest cuts from the meat store. We all love it, and it is also good for entertaining.

3 pounds boneless sirloin steak or London broil
2 teaspoons ground ginger
2 large garlic cloves, chopped
1 medium onion coarsely chopped
2 tablespoons sugar
½ cup soy sauce
¼ cup water

Mix all ingredients, except steak, in a pan that will comfortably hold the steak. Salt and pepper the steak, then place it in the marinade and turn to coat.

Let steak stand in marinade at room temperature for 3-4 hours, or cover and refrigerate overnight. Turn steak occasionally for both procedures.

To grill, wait until coals are grey before putting the steaks on the fire. Grill approximately 10 minutes on each side, or until desired doneness.

Let beef stand at least 10 minutes before carving.

Cheese Stuffed Pasta Shells with Tomato and Sausage Sauce
Serves 8

The tomato and sausage sauce is my standard sauce for spaghetti. When you're making this recipe, double the sauce and freeze half. The next time you're in the mood for spaghetti, dinner's in the freezer!

Tomato and Sausage Sauce

1 pound bulk sausage
1 medium onion, peeled and chopped
2 28-ounce cans of tomato, squished or chopped including
    juice
1 6-ounce can of tomato paste
2 large garlic cloves, crushed
3 bay leaves
2 tablespoons Italian seasoning
1 teaspoon salt
1 teaspoon sugar
¼ cup red wine
Freshly ground pepper

In a large sauce pan, brown sausage. Remove to a paper towel to drain. Pour out all but a tablespoon or less of fat. Add onions and simmer over medium heat until soft.

Add tomatoes, tomato paste, garlic, bay leaves, seasonings, and wine. Bring mixture to a boil. Stir in sausage. Reduce heat to a simmer and continue to cook for 20-30 minutes.

May be made ahead of time and reheated. Freezes well.

Squish your tomatoes!!!!! Why chop canned tomatoes when it is so much quicker, neater, and easier to squish them in your hand? Simply take the tomato out of the

can, hold it over the pot and squeeze! There is no cutting board or knife to clean. This is also a great way for children to help in the making of dinner.

Cheese Stuffed Pasta Shells

1 12-ounce package of jumbo pasta shells
2 pounds ricotta cheese
½ pound (8 ounces) mozzarella cheese, shredded
¼ cup grated Parmesan cheese
3 eggs
2 tablespoons chopped fresh parsley
Salt and pepper to taste

In a large pot of boiling water, cook shells until al dente. Drain, separate, and let cool on wax paper.

In a large mixing bowl, place ricotta, mozzarella, Parmesan, eggs, parsley, and salt and pepper. Stir until well blended.

Place several tablespoons of tomato ragout into the bottom of a 9 x 13 inch baking dish. Stuff cheese mixture into the shells with a tablespoon. Place stuffed shells in the baking dish. Cover with tomato and sausage sauce.

May be made several hours in advance up to this point. Or may be frozen.

Preheat oven to 350 degrees. Bake for 30 minutes or until bubbly.

This is a great dish to make in 2 separate containers. One for tonight's dinner, another in the freezer for a rainy day. This is also a super dinner to take to a friend. Dinners are a wonderful way to say you care. It is always one of the most appreciated gifts I ever give.

Cinco De Mayo

The Mexican holiday of Cinco de Mayo has become as much an American celebration as St. Patrick's Day. It seems everyone loves a good excuse to eat Mexican food and drink margaritas.

Hot Summer Salsa and chips

Fish Tacos

Mexican Beans

Spanish Rice

Mangos

Aniseed Cookies

The beans and the Spanish rice may be made ahead and reheated. Condiments for the fish tacos, such as grated cheese, lettuce and sliced jalapenos may also be done ahead. The cookies may be made a day ahead, or several weeks ahead and frozen.

Mangos are usually at the peak of their season the beginning of May. Serve them sliced with the meal, or place whole mangos in a bowl and let each diner slice their own.

Fish Tacos
Serves 6

Fish tacos are delicious, and such a refreshing change from chicken and beef.

In preparing fish tacos, use everything the same as you would for your favorite beef or chicken taco. The filling is the only item that changes.

3 tablespoons canola oil
1½ pounds white fish fillets (such as red snapper or catfish) cut into bite sized pieces
1 cup flour
2 tablespoons of your favorite taco seasoning mix
Taco shells or flour tortillas
Taco stuffings such as lettuce, tomato, and cheese

Prepare all stuffing ingredients for the tacos, except fish. We like to offer grated cheese, chopped tomatoes, shredded lettuce, jalapenos, black olives, salsa, avocado, and sour cream.

Heat taco shells and/or flour tortillas in a 300 degree oven.

Place flour in a shallow bowl. Stir in seasoning mix. Heat oil in a large skillet. Dredge fish pieces in flour mixture. Over medium-high heat, brown the fish pieces and cook until done, about 7 minutes. Season with salt and pepper.

For a little extra zest, try squeezing a wedge of fresh lime over your taco.

Taco Seasoning Mix
Enough for 1 pound of chicken or beef

My husband created this recipe one evening when the family was making tacos and we discovered there was no taco seasoning mix. The recipe has a medium kick and is also excellent on vegetables for fajitas.

3 teaspoons chili powder
1½ teaspoons ground cumin
1½ teaspoons salt
1 teaspoon dried chopped onions
1 teaspoon ground (cayenne) red pepper
¼ teaspoon garlic powder
¼ teaspoon onion salt

To make taco seasoning mix:
Mix all of the above spices in a small bowl.

To make meat for tacos:
In a medium skillet, brown 1 pound of chicken or ground beef. Pour off any excess oil or fat. Add ½ cup water. Stir in taco seasoning mix. Bring to a boil and continue to cook over medium heat until most liquid has evaporated. Meat is now ready to be used in taco shells.

Mexican Beans
Serves 6

This is a great side dish for baked pork or chicken, or for any Mexican entrée.

2 tablespoons olive oil
1 medium onion, chopped
1 garlic clove, minced
2 15-ounce cans black beans (3cups), partially drained
1 12-ounce can navy beans (1½ cups), partially drained
½ teaspoon ground cumin
2 jalapeno peppers, seeded and finely chopped
Juice of 1 lime
2 tablespoons rum
½ teaspoon salt
Freshly ground pepper to taste
Fresh cilantro, chopped (optional)

In a quart size pan heat the olive oil. Add the onions and sauté over medium heat until soft, add garlic and continue to cook. Add beans, cumin, peppers, lime juice, rum, salt and pepper. Simmer over low heat for approximately 10 minutes, or until flavors blend. Garnish with chopped, fresh cilantro, if desired.

May be made ahead of time and reheated.

BEWARE!! Not all jalapenos are created equal. Some jalapeno peppers have a slight kick, others are so hot they will make you sweat. When cooking with jalapeno or any chili pepper, be sure to go slow. Add about half the amount called for in the recipe, taste, then go ahead and add more depending on your cravings for spicy heat.

Spanish Rice
Serves 4-6

One of the nicest features about this rice dish is that is can be assembled ahead of time and bakes in the oven.

3 tablespoons olive oil
½ medium onion, chopped
1 garlic clove, minced
1 ½ cup chicken broth
1 14½-ounce can tomatoes, chopped with liquid
1 teaspoon salt
Freshly ground pepper to taste

Preheat oven to 300 degrees. In a 1½-2 quart enamel casserole (or any pot with a lid that can be heated on both the stove and in the oven) heat the oil, stir in the onions and garlic, and sauté over medium heat until soft. Stir in rice and continue to cook and stir until rice is translucent and begins to brown.

Add chicken broth, tomatoes, and salt and pepper to rice. The rice may be made several hours in advance up to this point.

Bring rice and chicken broth to a boil. Remove from heat. Cover and place in the oven. Bake 20-25 minutes or until the rice is tender and all the broth has been absorbed.

Spring III

Desserts

Angel Food Cake
Serves 8-10

Angel food cake is fun to make and it is so much better than the store-bought variety. If you have the time, try whipping the eggs by hand. There is something sensual in beating egg whites into stiff, glossy white peaks- to say nothing of the fact that it is an excellent exercise for arm muscles.

Cake flour must be used, as its low gluten content gives a particularly light, moist texture. It is also necessary to use a 10-inch angel food cake tube pan in which to bake. This recipe is adapted from <u>La Varenne Pratique</u> by Anne Willan.

1 cup cake flour
1½ cups sugar
1½ cups egg whites (about 12 large eggs)
1½ teaspoons cream of tartar
Pinch of salt
1 teaspoon vanilla extract

Preheat oven to 350 degrees. Sift the flour. Add about ⅓ of the sugar and sift the mixture twice again.

Whip the egg whites until foamy. Add the cream of tartar and salt and continue beating until the egg whites are stiff. Whip the remaining sugar into the egg whites, one tablespoon at a time. Continue whisking until the mixture is glossy and holds peaks. Beat in vanilla.

Fold in the flour in 3 batches. Transfer the batter to a 10-inch angel food cake pan that is NOT greased and floured. Bake 40-45 minutes or until cake is done. The cake is done when it shrinks from the sides of the pan and springs back when pressed.

Leave the cake to cool upside down in the pan so it does not shrink. (Rest the inverted pan on a jar or can so the air reaches the surface of the cake.)

We like to serve our angel food cake plain with fresh berries and ice cream. If you desire, however, the cake may be dusted with confectioners' sugar or coated with frosting.

If kept plain the cake may be stored in an airtight container for 2-3 days, or it may be frozen for up to 2 months.

Try making ice cream with leftover egg yolks. Angel food cake and homemade ice cream are an excellent combination.

Meringue Cake
with
Lemon Cream and Strawberry Sauce
Serve 6

For the Meringue Cake:
4 egg whites
½ teaspoon cream of tartar
1 teaspoon vanilla
¾ cup sugar

For the Lemon Cream
6 egg yolks, beaten
1 teaspoon unflavored gelatin
2/3 cup sugar
2 tablespoons butter
½ teaspoon grated lemon peel
⅓ cup lemon juice
¾ cup whipping cream

For the Strawberry Sauce
1 pound frozen strawberries
½ cup sugar
1 tablespoon raspberry liquor (optional)
Fresh strawberries for garnish if desired

To make the Meringue Cake:
　　Preheat oven to 300 degrees. Line 2 or 3 baking sheets
with parchment paper or brown paper. Draw three 7-inch
circles (about the size of a salad plate) on the paper.
　　Beat egg whites until frothy. Add cream of tartar. Beat
until peaks start to form. Add vanilla. Continue to beat and
gradually add sugar until all is incorporated and stiff peaks
are formed.
　　Divide the meringue evenly between the 3 circles.
With the back of a spoon or a spatula smooth meringue into

the circle pattern. Bake 45 minutes. Turn off the heat and let meringues dry in the oven for 3 hours, or overnight.

To make the Lemon Cream:

Beat egg yolks until light in color. In a medium saucepan, place egg yolks, gelatin, sugar, butter, lemon peel, lemon juice, and water. Over a medium heat cook and stir until mixture begins to boil. Cook an additional 2 minutes. Remove from heat. Cover mixture with waxed paper and cool in refrigerator until chilled. Beat cream until soft peaks form. Fold whipped cream into cool lemon mixture.

To assemble cake:

Place one meringue circle on cake platter. Spread half of the lemon mixture over it. Top with a second meringue circle. Spread remaining lemon cream on circle. Top with final circle. Cover loosely. Chill several hours, or overnight.

To make Strawberry Sauce:

In a medium saucepan, place strawberries to defrost. Mash berries and add sugar. Bring mixture to a boil and cook about 5 minutes or until sauce begins to thicken. Remove from heat. Skim off any foam. Stir in liquor if desired.

Serve with cake. Sauce may be drizzled over cake or puddle on the side. Garnish with fresh strawberries, if desired.

Strawberry-Rhubarb Ice Cream
Makes about 1 ½ pints

There are no better flavors to usher in spring than strawberries and rhubarb. Strawberries grown in the U.S. usually begin to appear in the grocers around the end of February or the beginning of March. Next to the berries, the early spring vegetable rhubarb can often be found. The sweet-tart taste of the two is sure to wake-up your senses to spring and all the new flavors and colors that await you in the months ahead.

3 cups cleaned, sliced strawberries
1 cup peeled, diced rhubarb
1 cup sugar
2 cups milk
4 egg yolks, slightly beaten
½ teaspoon vanilla

In a medium saucepan, combine strawberries, rhubarb, and sugar. Bring the mixture to a boil. Skim off any foam. Continue to boil and stir mixture until all is soft, about 5-7 minutes. Cool.

In a separate saucepan, scald milk. Reduce heat to low. Slowly add beaten egg yolks in a steady stream, stirring constantly. When all the egg yolks have been incorporated, continue to cook and stir over low heat until mixture begins to thicken and coats a spoon. Cool.

When egg and milk mixture has cooled, stir in strawberry mixture. Add vanilla.

Freeze in an ice cream maker, following manufacturer's directions.

There is something that is associated with a homemade dessert that evokes among all of us a sense of comfort and well being – it is a gift of love.
- Nancy Silverton, 20th century American chef

Chocolate Torte
Serves 10-12

A torte is a rich, rather heavy cake that makes use of ground nuts (usually pecans) instead of flour. Tortes are especially suited for entertaining in that they may be made the day ahead, refrigerated, and they taste just as good as the day they were made.

6 ounces bittersweet chocolate
1 cup pecans
3 tablespoons flour
¾ cup butter (1½ sticks), softened
¾ cup sugar
4 egg yolks
6 egg whites

Preheat oven to 350 degrees. Line a 10-inch round cake pan with parchment or wax paper. Grease and flour the paper.

Melt the chocolate in the top of a double broiler or in the microwave. Place pecans and flour in a blender or food processor and pulverize them.

In a medium mixing bowl, cream the butter and sugar together until light and fluffy. Add the egg yolks, one at a time, beating after each addition. Stir in melted chocolate and pulverized pecan mixture.

In a separate bowl, beat egg whites until stiff. Fold egg whites into chocolate mixture. Pour into prepared pan. Bake for 30 minutes or until cake tests done. Let cake cool. Turn out of pan, carefully remove parchment paper, then frost.

Chocolate Frosting

¼ cup Kahlua Liquor
¼ cup sugar
3½ ounces bittersweet chocolate
1 cup heavy cream

In a small saucepan, combine Kahlua, sugar and chocolate. Cook over medium heat, stirring, until chocolate is melted and sugar is dissolved. Let mixture cool, stirring occasionally, for 5 minutes.

Whip cream until stiff. Fold into chocolate mixture. Chill frosting for 20 minutes or until it is of spreading consistency.

Chocolate Covered Strawberries

Chocolate covered strawberries are a great dessert for lunch or dinner. They are as beautiful to look at as they are delicious to eat. For an interesting presentation, try dipping some strawberries in white chocolate and others in dark chocolate.

Always have the strawberries at room temperature before dipping. Cold berries will cause the chocolate to get hard. When melting chocolate, the room temperature should be between 65 and 70 degrees with as little humidity as possible.

1-1½ pounds strawberries, stems on, room temperature
2 cups semi-sweet chocolate chips, or 12 ounces semi-sweet chocolate

Cove a baking sheet with wax paper.

Melt the chocolate in the top of a double broiler. Stir constantly while chocolate is melting. Once the chocolate has melted, turn off the heat, but leave the top of the double broiler with the chocolate sitting over the hot water.

Dip each strawberry into the chocolate and place on wax paper. When all the strawberries have been dipped, refrigerate them until chocolate hardens, about 20 minutes.

Strawberry Tree
Another interesting way to serve strawberries for a buffet is to make a strawberry tree. Place a Styrofoam cone on a cake plate. Using toothpicks, cove the cone with fresh strawberries, placing the stem side of the berry into the cone. Sift powdered sugar over the cone.

Strawberry Pie
Serves 6

4 cups cleaned and sliced strawberries
1 cup sugar
¼ cup flour
½ teaspoon cinnamon
dash salt
2 tablespoons butter
pastry for a two-crust 9-inch pie (p.145)

Preheat oven to 425 degrees. In a medium mixing bowl place strawberries, sugar, flour, cinnamon and salt. Stir until well combined.

Line a pie pan with pastry crust. Fill with strawberry mixture. Slice butter on top of strawberries. Place on the top crust. Seal and crimp edges. Cut slits in top crust to vent steam.

Bake 15 minutes. Reduce heat to 350 degrees and bake an additional 30 minutes or until center begins to bubble. Cool on rack.

To seal the top and bottom of pie crusts together, try brushing the rim of the bottom pie crust with a partially beaten egg white. Then cover with top crust. The egg white works as a glue to seal the crusts together. Remaining egg white may be brushed on top layer of pie crust to help it brown.

To make a Strawberry-Rhubarb Pie, use 2 cups strawberries and 2 cups peeled and diced rhubarb in place of the 4 cups of strawberries called for in the above recipe.

Kiwi Pie
Serves 6

Although kiwi is available year-round, it is at its peak in the late winter and early spring. This is a delicious fruit pie, and is made even better with a scoop of vanilla ice cream. Serve the pie warm, at room temperature, or cold.

1 pound kiwi, (about 5), peeled and sliced into ¼ inch
 circles
Juice of ½ lime
½ cup sugar
2 large eggs
3 tablespoons sugar
2 tablespoons flour
1 teaspoon vanilla extract
⅓ cup cream or milk
pastry for one 9-inch pie crust (p.145)
powdered sugar for dusting top (optional)

Preheat oven to 375 degrees. Place kiwi in a mixing bowl. Add the ½ cup sugar and lime juice. Toss so that fruit is covered. In a separate bowl, beat the eggs and the 3 tablespoons sugar. Beat in flour, vanilla, and cream. Line a 9 –inch pie pan with dough. Put kiwi in the pie shell and cover with egg mixture. Flute edges of pastry crust. Bake approximately 30 minutes or until nicely browned and pie has set. Remove from oven and dust with powdered sugar. Let cool several minutes on rack before serving. May be made a day in advance and kept refrigerated.

The best way to eat kiwi is to cut it in half and use a spoon to eat it right out of the shell.

Lemon, Coconut, and Chocolate Tart
Serves 8-10

Pastry for one 9-inch pie (p.145)
3 ounces bittersweet chocolate
½ cup flaked coconut
2 large eggs
½ cup sugar (divided)
Juice of 1 large lemon

Preheat oven to 425 degrees. Line a 9-inch quiche pan with pastry shell. Prick shell with a fork. Bake tart shell about 10 minutes or until it is lightly browned. Remove from oven and cool.

Melt chocolate in the top of a double broiler or microwave. With a pastry brush, paint melted chocolate over bottom of tart shell. Sprinkle coconut over the chocolate.

In the top of a double broiler, beat egg yolks and half of the sugar (1/4 cup) until pale yellow. Add lemon juice. Heat the double broiler over medium heat, constantly whisking mixture until it is thick enough to coat the back of a spoon. Set aside.

In a medium mixing bowl, beat egg whites until soft peaks form. Slowly add the remaining ¼ cup of sugar and continue beating until egg whites form stiff peaks. Carefully fold egg whites into yolk mixture. Spread over chocolate and coconut. Refrigerate at least one hour before serving.

"Used as food in southeast Asia and Polynesia from the earliest times, the coconut was 'discovered' by Marco Polo, who described 'the Pharaoh's nut' as a fruit full of flavour, sweet as sugar, and white as milk, providing at the same time both food and drink."
- Larousse Gastronomique

Summer

Summer sizzles. The grill sears our food. The peppers burn our mouths. It's hot and sweltering.

We reach for minty concoctions to cool our thirsts.We want ice cream and fresh iced tea. We wait with hot, wet coins in our hands for the bells of the snow-cone man.

It's too hot to cook and we're usually too tired. Summer meals are simple and often best cold. There is plenty of fresh, local produce to make our mouths water.

We need lots of basil and sliced, home-grown tomatoes to soothe our souls.

It's berry picking time, and anything goes. Fruit pies for breakfast, grilled sausages for dinner, and a picnic lunch by the pool.

Life and food are good in the summer.

Summer I

Appetizers

Soups

Salads

Breads

Breakfast Foods

A Cool Graduation Lunch Buffet

When my son graduated from high school, we decided to have a lunch buffet to celebrate the event. Providing a cold lunch for a crowd of 40 or so is not too difficult a task. Colorful vegetables and fruits make this a spectacular buffet table.

Crudités
Assorted Cheeses
Assortment of Olives
Basket of Breads, Rolls, and Crackers
Baked Ham
Seviche
Strawberry Tree
Sliced Cantaloupe and Honeydew

Red Chocolate Cake

The cake or cakes may be made several weeks in advance. Bake the cake but do not frost. The seviche and the strawberry tree can be made a day ahead. The melons may also be sliced a day in advance as well as preparing the crudités. The dip or dips for the crudités may also be made 24 to 48 hours before the party.

Make sure there are rolls in the bread basket to make ham sandwiches. Sliced French or Italian bread is the perfect accompaniment for cheeses.

Crudités

Crudités- a wonderful word for raw vegetables that are dipped in a sauce. The crudités may be as simple as celery and carrot sticks with bottled ranch dressing, to the elaborate, exotic baby vegetables with several homemade sauces. The purpose is the same: to provide a healthy snack before dining.

Use a variety of vegetables for a spectacular presentation and be creative in how you present the veggies: a basket, large trays, or a hollowed-out giant zucchini.

Our favorite dips for crudités are:
Mayonnaise Verte
Blue Cheese Salad Dressing
Sweet Mustard Dill Sauce

We like serving all three with a wide variety of vegetables for an interesting combination of tastes, textures, and colors.

Our favorite vegetables for crudités are:

Asparagus spears. Blanched until crisp
Baby Artichokes, cooked and chilled
Beets, cooked and sliced if large, whole if small
Broccoli tops, blanched or raw
Brussels Sprouts, cooked and chilled
Carrot Sticks
Celery Sticks
Cucumber Slices
Hard Boiled Eggs (yes we know they are not a vegetable!)
Green Beans, whole and blanched until crisp, chilled
Mushrooms
Pea Pods
Bell Pepper Strips, red, green, and yellow
Potatoes (new or baby), boiled and chilled
Scallions
Tomatoes, Cherry or Pear
Zucchini Spears

Mayonnaise Verte
Makes ½ Cup

½ cup packed fresh flat-leafed parsley leaves
2 tablespoons olive oil
2 tablespoons lemon juice
1 teaspoon Dijon mustard
½ cup mayonnaise
Salt and pepper to taste

Wash and dry parsley leaves. Place in a blender or food processor with olive oil, lemon juice and mustard. Puree until smooth. Stir puree into mayonnaise and season with salt and pepper.

May be prepared several days in advance and kept refrigerated.

Seviche
Serves 6

Seviche is a Latin American dish where raw fish is marinated in lime juice. The acid in the lime "cooks" the fish by acting on the tissue so the flesh is whitened and its texture stiffened while retaining a fresh, clean flavor. It is a refreshing summer appetizer or first course. Serve with tortilla chips.

Freshness of the fish is vital to seviche. Prime choices for marinating are firm fish like sea bass, snapper, or scallops.

1 pound fresh, raw fish (skin and bones removed), cut into ½ inch dice
1¼ cup fresh squeezed lime juice (5-8 limes)
½ cup chopped red onion (about ½ an onion)
2 jalapeno peppers, seeded and minced
1 teaspoon coarse salt
Freshly ground pepper to taste
2 medium red tomatoes, cut into ½ inch dice
½ cup diced yellow or green bell pepper
2 tablespoons chopped fresh cilantro leaves

In a medium bowl, place lime juice, onion, jalapeno peppers, fish, salt, and pepper. Stir to coat. Cover and refrigerate at least 5 hours and up to a day ahead.

Before serving, place chopped tomatoes, diced bell peppers, and cilantro in a small bowl. Spoon fish into tomato mixture, adding enough of the lime juice to make a salsa-like consistency.

Refrigerate until ready to serve. Serve cold with tortilla chips.

"Time is but the stream I go a-fishing in."
- **Henry David Thoreau, Walden**

Eggplant Appetizer
Serves 12

This has become one of my favorite appetizer recipes because it can be made several days in advance, or frozen, and it seems to keep forever. I usually make a batch at the end of summer when the eggplant is at its peak, then I freeze some to have on hand during the holidays.

⅓ cup olive oil
1 medium eggplant, with skin, finely chopped
1 large onion, chopped
½ cup mushrooms, chopped (optional)
⅓ cup green bell pepper, chopped
2 cloves of garlic, minced
½ cup stuffed green olives, chopped
¼ cup ripe olives, chopped
¼ cup cappers, drained
3 tablespoons pine nuts
1 6-ounce can tomato paste
⅓ cup water
2 tablespoons red wine vinegar
1 tablespoon sugar
2 teaspoons chopped fresh oregano
½ teaspoon dried oregano
1 teaspoon salt
½ teaspoon freshly ground pepper

In a large saucepan, heat oil over medium heat. Add eggplant, onion, mushroom, green pepper, and garlic. Stir, reduce heat to low and simmer covered for 10 minutes. Add remaining ingredients, mix well and simmer covered, for 25 minutes, stirring occasionally. Eggplant should be cooked but not overly soft. May be made several days in advance and kept refrigerated or may be frozen.

Serve at room temperature with crackers, cocktail pumpernickel.

Bruschetta

Serves 6

The secret to this recipe is to let the tomatoes drain and intensify their wonderful flavor. The recipe is from a friend and former neighbor, Mary Wenclawski's.

1½ pound fresh tomatoes, finely chopped
1 teaspoon salt
1 tablespoon minced fresh basil   2 - 3 garlic
2 tablespoons minced fresh parsley   cloves, chopped
¼ cup olive oil
Ground pepper to taste
One loaf of French or Italian bread, cut into ½ inch thick
    slices, lightly toasted

Place chopped tomatoes in a colander and toss with salt. Let drain one hour. Stir occasionally.

Place drained tomatoes in a medium-sized serving bowl and mix with all remaining ingredients. Serve cool or at room temperature over toasted bread slices.

It is not necessary to remove the skin of the tomato for Bruschettas or Salsas.

Hot Summer Salsa
Makes about 1 quart

The better the tomato, the better the salsa.

2 ½ pounds tomatoes, coarsely chopped (about 4 cups)
1 medium onion, chopped
3 jalapeno peppers, seeded and finely chopped
2 tablespoons fresh cilantro, chopped
1 teaspoon coarse salt
Juice of ½ a lime

In a large bowl mix all ingredients. Refrigerate until cool. Serve with chips or on tacos.

The salsa is hot. You might want to make it with one jalapeno and add more according to taste.

Remember that not all jalapenos are created equal. Some are very hot, some are not so hot, and there is no way to tell the difference between the two without tasting them.

Homemade salsas are best eaten the day they are made. They will taste fine after 24 hours, they just won't look as pretty.

The Good Life

There is nothing finer in the summer than bar-b-que, local corn on the cob, and fresh fruit for dessert. It is truly living the good life.

Cold Cucumber Soup

Bar-B-Que Chicken
Corn on the Cob
Coleslaw

Meringue Cookies with Peaches and Berries

People who eat at home have significantly higher levels of several types of cancer-fighting carotenoids than people who eat out once a week or more, according to a recent National Cancer Institute analysis of the diets of more than 22,000 Americans.
- **Cooking Light Magazine, July/August 1998**

Cold Cucumber and Potato Soup
Serves 4

Similar to a vichyssoise, only more refreshing.

1 shallot, minced
1 tablespoon butter
1 large potato, peeled and minced
2½ cup chicken stock
1 tablespoon fresh parsley, chopped
1 teaspoon salt
Freshly ground pepper to taste
2 medium cucumbers, peeled, seeded, roughly chopped

In a medium saucepan, melt the butter over low heat. Add shallots and sauté until soft. Add minced potato, chicken stock, parsley, and salt and pepper. Bring to a boil. Reduce heat to a simmer and continue to simmer until potatoes are cooked and begin to fall apart. Remove from heat.

Place potato/stock mixture into blender or food processor, along with the chopped cucumber. Puree until smooth.

Place soup in container and refrigerate several hours, or until cold.

Serve cold. Garnish with a dollop of sour cream if desired.

Cream of Zucchini Soup
Serves 4

The zucchini is a wonderful, versatile vegetable. Its reputation, however, is not quite so glorious. Most people turn their noses up when you mention the word zucchini. Grocery stores have even started calling the summer squash, "Italian Squash" rather than, "zucchini".

Zucchini is often thought of as the only vegetable your neighbor gives you from their garden. Known to grow to the size of a baseball bat almost overnight, large zucchini are not very tasty. However, when the squash is picked at a young age, about 4-5 inches, the vegetable is truly delicious. Try zucchini, or Italian squash, thinly sliced and sautéed in a little olive oil, add salt and pepper and a few fresh herbs. Sprinkle grated Parmesan cheese on top. It is a great summer side dish.

This soup is very good both hot and cold. It is a great picnic soup when served cold. This recipe doubles well, the soup must just be pureed in batches rather than all at once.

1 pound young zucchini, trim stem and flowering end
2 tablespoons butter
2 tablespoons shallots, finely chopped
1 clove garlic, minced
1¾ cups chicken broth
½ cup cream
1 teaspoon mild curry powder
½ teaspoon salt

Slice zucchini very thin. In a medium saucepan, heat butter, add sliced zucchini, shallots, and garlic. Reduce heat to medium-low. Cover and simmer about 10 minutes or until vegetables are very soft. Stir occasionally. Do not let mixture brown. When vegetables are soft, remove from heat.

In a blender or food processor place chicken stock, cream, curry, and salt. Add cooked zucchini mixture. Puree until smooth. To serve hot, return soup to saucepan and reheat. To serve cold, place soup in refrigerator for several hours or until well chilled.

If doubling the recipe, add the liquid ingredients and spices to the saucepan with cooked zucchini, then puree in batches.

Many soups can be served hot *or* cold. Spinach, cucumber, and zucchini are good examples. Remember you need a little extra salt with cold soups to help bring out the flavor.

Gazpacho
Serves 4

This cold Spanish soup has as many variations as there are varieties of vegetables. This recipe is one of my favorites, another from friend Mary Wenclawski. Feel free to alter the amount of vegetables in the recipe depending on availability and your own personal taste.

The soup is best made several hours in advance so the flavors have a chance to develop. Serve plain or topped with fresh veggies and a dollop of sour cream.

½ cup V-8 juice
½ cup cucumber, peeled and chopped
½ cup green bell pepper, chopped
½ cup onion, chopped
2 large ripe tomatoes, chopped
2 tablespoons lemon juice
1 tablespoon vegetable oil
½ teaspoon salt
¼ teaspoon Tabasco Sauce
Chopped cucumbers, tomatoes, and bell peppers for garnish
Sour cream or yogurt, optional

Place all ingredients (except the vegetables for garnish) in a blender or food processor and puree until almost smooth. Refrigerate for several hours, up to 24. Garnish with freshly chopped vegetables and a dollop of sour cream or plain yogurt.

"I always see to it that I have made too much Gazpacho. It ripens well when kept chilled, and it is a soul-satisfying think to drink, chilled, midway in a torrid morning. It is also one of the world's best breakfasts for unfortunates who are badly hung over."
- **M.F.K. Fisher, <u>The Art of Eating</u>**

Blue Cheese Salad Dressing
Makes about 1 cup

3 ounces blue cheese
2 tablespoons hot water
⅓ cup mayonnaise
⅓ cup sour cream
¼ teaspoon Tabasco Sauce
Salt and pepper

Place cheese in a small bowl. Break apart with a fork, add hot water, stir until nearly smooth. Stir in mayonnaise, sour cream and Tabasco. Add salt and pepper to taste.

This dressing will keep, refrigerated, up to one week.

"Everybody is a story. When I was a child, people sat around the kitchen tables and told their stories. We don't do that so much anymore. Sitting around the table and telling stories is not just a way of passing time. It is the way the wisdom gets passed along. The stuff that helps us to live a life worth remembering. Despite the awesome powers of technology, many of us still do not live very well. We may need to listen to each other's stories once again."
- **Rachel Naomi Remen, M.D., <u>Kitchen Table Wisdom: Stories that Heal</u>**

Raspberry Salad Dressing
Makes 1 pint

This wonderful salad dressing is delicious lightly tossed over mixed greens. It is spectacular, however, when a few slices of red onion, crumbled blue cheese or goat cheese, and a few edible flowers are added. Fresh raspberries are also a welcome addition.

½ cup raspberry vinegar
½ cup olive oil
½ cup vegetable oil
½ cup pure maple syrup
1 tablespoon Dijon mustard
1 teaspoon dried tarragon leaves
Dash salt

Whisk ingredients together until well blended. Pour enough dressing over salad so that leaves are lightly coated when tossed.

Refrigerate the remaining dressing. Dressing will keep for several weeks in the refrigerator.

Zucchini Bread

Makes 2 large loaves

This bread is excellent for breakfast spread with cream cheese, it is good for lunch with a salad, and delicious at dinner with grilled food.

3 eggs
2 cups sugar
2 cups grated raw zucchini
1 cup vegetable oil
1 tablespoon vanilla
3 cups flour
1 tablespoon ground cinnamon
1 teaspoon salt
1 teaspoon baking soda
¼ teaspoon baking powder
1 cup chopped pecans or walnuts

Preheat oven to 350 degrees. Grease two 4x5x3 inch loaf pans.

In a medium mixing bowl, beat eggs until light and foamy. Add sugar, zucchini, oil, and vanilla. Mix lightly, but well.

In another bowl, sift together the flour, cinnamon, salt, baking soda, and baking powder. Add flour mixture to zucchini/egg mixture. Stir to blend. Stir in nuts. Divide batter between the two loaf pans.

Bake approximately 1 hour or until done. Bread is done when a cake tester, inserted into the center of the loaf, comes out clean. Cool on rack. Freezes well.

Anyone who has a vegetable garden, or lives near someone with a vegetable garden, should have a recipe for Zucchini Bread.

Father's Day Brunch

We like to do an early Father's Day celebration and cook something on the grill. This gives Dad the rest of the day to play golf, take a nap, or do whatever else he'd like.

Grilled Sausages
Mom's Egg and Cheese Breakfast Soufflé
Blueberry Coffee Cake
Fresh Fruit

There are so many different types of sausages available at specialty stores and supermarkets. It is fun to try an assortment. Of course, I can never keep track of which one is which while they are cooking. Everyone, however, always has a good laugh trying to guess.

We have found it best to parboil sausages before grilling them. To parboil, poke holes in sausage casing with a fork and place in simmering water for 20 minutes. Do not boil, keep water at a low simmer. Remove sausages and they are ready to be grilled. Since the parboiling cooks the sausage meat, the sausages just need to be browned over a medium-hot grill; this should finish the cooking process. We use this same technique for ribs. (Parboil for 20 minutes then grill). The sausages may also be parboiled a day in advance and kept refrigerated.

The coffee cake may be made one day in advance, although my children like it warm, just out of the oven. It may also be made a week or two in advance and frozen. Defrost and heat through in the oven.

The soufflé needs to be made the day before and cooked that morning.

The fresh fruit should also be peeled and chopped the morning of the brunch. Use whatever fresh fruit is in season and featured at the market that week. I think mixing colors in a bowl of fruit is just as important as mixing flavors. Add a squeeze of lime for a little extra zest and to help prevent the fruit from turning brown.

Blueberry Coffee Cake
Serves 6

¾ cup sugar
4 tablespoons butter
1 egg
1 cup plain low fat yogurt or 1 cup buttermilk
½ cup milk
2 cups flour
4 teaspoons baking powder
½ teaspoon salt
1 cup blueberries

Topping:
3 tablespoons sugar
1 teaspoon cinnamon

Preheat the oven to 350 degrees. Grease an 8-inch square baking pan or a cake pan. In a mixing bowl, cream together sugar and butter. Add egg and beat until mixed. Add milk and yogurt (or buttermilk) and stir until combined

In a separate bowl sift together the flour, baking powder, and salt. Add to milk and egg mixture and stir. Stir in 1 cup blueberries. Pour into baking pan. In a small bowl mix sugar and cinnamon together for topping. Pour over coffee cake. Bake for 40 minutes or until brown and cake begins to pull away from the pan.

Substitute: Buttermilk and plain yogurt may be interchanged in most recipes.

Buttermilk or Yogurt????
One cup of 1% buttermilk has 100 calories.
One cup of 1% plain yogurt has 140 calories.
My family cannot taste any difference between the coffee cake baked with buttermilk and the coffee cake baked with yogurt. It's your choice.

Breakfast Fruit Tart in a Pan
Serves 3

This delicious, beautiful, and very appealing breakfast is somewhere in-between a crepe, a pancake, and a tart. However, it is much easier to prepare than any of the three.

It is the perfect romantic breakfast for a lazy summer morning. And, if the children are around use a 12" pan instead of the recommended 10" and double the recipe. (The cooking time will be a little longer). Everyone loves this tart. This is also a great way to use summer fruit.

4 tablespoons butter
½ cup flour
½ cup milk
2 eggs, lightly beaten
Pinch ground nutmeg
2 tablespoons powdered sugar
Juice of 1 lemon
3 tablespoons apricot or peach jam, heated in microwave to melt
2-3 large peaches, peeled and sliced*

Preheat oven to 425 degrees. Place butter in a 10-inch oven proof skillet. Place the skillet in the oven to melt the butter.

In a medium bowl, lightly mix flour, milk, eggs and nutmeg. Batter should be a little lumpy. Remove skillet from oven when butter has melted. Pour batter into skillet. Do not stir. Place skillet back in over and bake 15-20 minutes or until golden brown.

Remove from oven and sprinkle with powdered sugar and lemon juice. Spread jam over. Top with peaches. Return to oven and bake until sugar begins to brown, 3-5 minutes. Slice into wedges and serve.

*You can substitute many fruits for the peaches. Try bananas, blueberries and strawberries, apples, nectarines, or plums.

Breakfast is the most important meal of the day. Why not make it the most delicious and the most romantic as well?

Frittata with Cheese, Potato, and Red Onion
Serves 4-6

Frittate are often described as Italian omelets. Unlike the omelets we know, however, frittate are easy to make. Frittate are cooked very slowly in a skillet, then run under the broiler to finish. There is no flipping, turning, or folding.

A frittata may be sliced and put neatly between two layers of bread for a sandwich, or cut into a pie-shaped wedge and eaten by hand like a quiche. They are equally good for breakfast, lunch, or dinner, and may be eaten hot or at room temperature. Frittate are great on picnics, in a box lunch, or served as an appetizer at a dinner party.

1 10-inch skillet with a flameproof handle. A cast iron skillet works well.

¾ pound red potatoes (about 3 medium)
2 teaspoons olive oil
1 small red onion, peeled and thinly sliced
1 clove garlic, minced
6 eggs
1 cup (4 ounces) freshly grated cheese (Parmesan, Swiss, or your favorite)
1 tablespoon chopped fresh basil leaves, or 1 teaspoon dried basil
1 teaspoon chopped fresh thyme leaves, or ½ teaspoon dried thyme
½ teaspoon salt
Freshly grated pepper

In a small pot bring salted water to a boil. Add potatoes and cook until tender when pierced with a fork (about 10 minutes). Remove potatoes from water and let cool. Slice potatoes about ¼ inch thick. Set aside.

Heat olive oil in skillet over medium heat. Add onions and garlic and sauté until soft. Remove from heat.

In a medium bowl whisk eggs. Add grated cheese, basil, thyme, salt and pepper to taste.

Return skillet with onions to stove, bring to a medium heat.. Add eggs and cheese. Place sliced potatoes on top. Reduce heat to low. Do NOT stir. Turn oven broiler on.

Continue to cook egg mixture on stove over low heat until the eggs have set and thickened and only the surface in runny (about 5-7 minutes). At this point place the skillet under the broiler and remove as soon as the "face" of the frittata sets and begins to brown. Remove frittata from skillet and let cool slightly before cutting.

Summer II

Entrees

Side Dishes

The Magic of Picnics

Who doesn't love a family picnic? We seem to have the best conversations and I've learned more about my children on picnics than at any other event, place or time I remember.

Picnics are truly magical. Maybe it's the picnic blanket that makes the magic, perhaps it enables us to converse more freely- to share our thoughts, a joke, or a good story. Or maybe it's just being in the outdoors, the magical spirit of the wind and sun making us feel happy and relaxed.

Whatever the reason, every picnic I've ever been on has had a special magic. There are no telephones or televisions to interrupt conversations, and meals never seem to be hurried.

Family picnics are wonderful and an essential part of the summer ritual. Picnics do not need to be planned, nor do they have to be far from home. Spread an old bedspread out in the backyard on nice summer evening and announce that dinner is a picnic. The children will laugh and call you crazy, but it will be a fun-filled, memorable evening.

Kids' sporting events are almost always held at dinner time. Change the routine and picnic. Take dinner to the field before the game. There is almost always a place to picnic: on the field, at a vacant lot near the field, or tailgate in the car. It's a wonderful experience. The kids will have fun and the food always tastes so much better at a picnic.

Don't wait for a special occasion, picnic today!

Crudités

**Turkey, Cheese, and Vidalia Onion Pie with
Strawberry Mango Salsa
Roasted Green Beans**

Butterscotch Brownies

Turkey, Cheese, and Vidalia Onion Pie
with
Strawberry Mango Salsa
Makes 2, 9-inch pies
8 Servings

Pastry for 2, 9-inch pie crusts(p.145)
1 pound cooked turkey or chicken, cut into ½ inch cubes
    (about 4 cups)
4 medium Vidalia onions*, about 1¼ pounds, sliced thin
1 tablespoon olive oil
½ tablespoon butter
1 pound Monterey Jack cheese, shredded and divided
1 cup grated dry Monterey Jack Cheese**, divided

    Preheat oven to 375 degrees. Line two 9-inch pie pans with crust. Refrigerate until ready to use.
    Cube turkey, slice onions, and grate cheese. Set aside in individual bowls until ready to use.
    In a medium skillet melt the butter and olive oil. Add onions and sauté over low heat (covered and stirring occasionally) until onions are soft and just starting to brown, about 15 minutes.
    To assemble the first pie, spread half of the onions over the pie crust. Top with half of the cubed turkey. Salt and pepper to taste. Top turkey with half of the Monterey Jack cheese. Finish by sprinkling ½ cup dry Monterey Jack on top. Repeat for second pie.
    The pies may be made ahead to this point. Cover and refrigerate until ready to bake, up to 24 hours.
    Bake for one hour.
    When the pie is finished baking, let cool on a rack for several minutes before slicing. Each pie will provide 4 servings.
    Pie may also be frozen after baking. Defrost then warm in the oven before serving.

Delicious when accompanied by Strawberry Mango Salsa.

* Vidalia onions are a sweet onion from Georgia that are available in late spring and early summer. Plain yellow onions may be substituted.
** Dry Monterey Jack Cheese is a California cheese that is now available in many supermarkets. Parmesan cheese may be substituted.

Strawberry Mango Salsa

3 cups strawberries, cleaned and cut in half, quarter if large
1 mango, skinned and cut into bite-sized pieces
3 tablespoons raspberry vinegar
1 tablespoon sugar

Place strawberries and mango pieces in a medium bowl. In a small bowl, whisk together the vinegar and the sugar. Pour over fruit. Stir to coat.

Cover and refrigerate several hours to marinate flavors. Serve on the side of Turkey, Cheese, and Vidalia onion Pie.

Also good as a condiment for grilled poultry or fish.

Everything is good in its season.
-Italian Proverb

Roasted Green Beans

Allow approximately one handful of raw green beans per serving.

Preheat oven to 375 degrees. Clean beans. Remove ends, but leave whole. Dry on a paper towel.

Place beans on a cookie sheet. Drizzle with olive oil and toss to coat. Sprinkle beans with salt (coarse salt preferred).

Bake for approximately 30 minutes, or until tender. Serve at room temperature. May be made 5 to 6 hours in advance.

Though a man lives a thousand years twice over, but he doesn't find contentment, what's the use?
-   **Ecclesiastes 6:6**

Pesto

Makes about 1 cup
Enough to sauce 1 pound of pasta

Pesto tastes of summer. It is wonderful served over pasta. Or, try a dollop of pesto on slices of tomatoes and mozzarella. A tablespoon or two livens-up a plate of spaghetti sauce. Best of all, it is fun and easy to make your own.

1 cup tightly packed fresh basil leaves
3 – 4 cloves of garlic, minced
⅓ cup pine nuts or chopped walnuts
1 cup freshly grated Parmesan cheese
¾ cup olive oil
dash of salt and pepper

Place basil leaves, garlic, nuts and cheese in a food processor. Process until well mixed. Puree mixture and begin to add oil slowly in a steady stream until all is added and sauce is well blended. Season with salt and pepper. To serve, pour over cooked pasta and toss.

Pesto will keep in refrigerator for several days and freezes very well.

"Pesto is the sauce the Genoese invented as a vehicle for the fragrance of a basil like no other, their own. Olive oil, garlic, pine nuts, butter and grated cheese are the only other components. Pesto is never cooked, or heated, and while it may on occasion do good things for a vegetable soup, it has just one great role: to be the most seductive of all sauces for pasta."
- **Marchlla Hazan, <u>Essential of Classic Italian Cooking</u>**

Garden-Fresh Spaghetti Sauce
Serves 4 – 6

The fresh herbs and tomatoes help make this a wonderful, light summer meal – but it may also be frozen and eaten on a cold winter evening when it surely will bring back memories of summer past.

5 pounds fresh (preferably local or home-grown)
    tomatoes, skinned and coarsely chopped
2 tablespoons olive oil
1 large onion, peeled and chopped
1 small red bell pepper, seeded and chopped
1 small green bell pepper, seeded and chopped
1 jalapeno pepper, seeded and finely chopped
1 large clove garlic, minced
2 tablespoons chopped fresh oregano leaves
2 tablespoons chopped fresh basil leaves
1 teaspoon chopped fresh thyme leaves
1 teaspoon chopped fresh rosemary leaves
1 teaspoon sugar
1 teaspoon salt
Freshly ground pepper to taste

Skin and chop tomatoes, place in a bowl and set aside. In a large pot heat oil, add onions, peppers and garlic and sauté over medium heat until soft. Add tomatoes, herbs, sugar, salt and pepper. Bring to a boil, then reduce heat to simmer. Continue to simmer over low heat for 45 – 60 minutes. Stirring occasionally.

Serve over pasta and serve with plenty of freshly grated Parmesan cheese.

To skin tomatoes: Place tomatoes in a large bowl or sink. Cover with boiling water. Let stand several minutes. Drain water and rinse with cool water. Skin should peel off easily with a knife.

Memorial Day Dinner with the Family

Memorial Day heralds the arrival of summer. More often than not, however, our Memorial Day Weekend is centered around end of school activities and studying for exams. There rarely seems time to get away or have a big celebration.

We hang our flags and usually have a nice, quiet family cookout. This menu is easy to prepare and gets us in the mood for the summer that we know can not be far away.

Sliced Tomato and Mozzarella, drizzled with olive oil and balsamic vinegar
Ribs on the Barbie with a Green Chili Kick
Corn on the Cob
Steamed Spinach

Nectarine and Peach Crisp

Bar-B-Que Chicken
Serves 4 – 6

Nothing beats a good Bar-B-Que . Just ask anyone from the South. Everyone has a favorite recipe. Some like a lot of vinegar, some a lot of tomato, and a lot of preference depends upon which part of the South from which you hail. We developed our favorite bar-b-que recipe while living in Atlanta. It is easily changed to suit personal taste. Try a little less cayenne if you like your sauce without a kick. Add more or less vinegar depending on whether or not you like a thick or thin bar-b-que. Add more ketchup if you like tomato flavor.

Another secret to a good chicken or pork bar-b-que is to parboil the meat in the sauce before cooking the food on the grill. This technique infuses the taste of the sauce in the food, keeps the meat moist, helps ensure the food will be done and cuts down on grilling time. By parboiling you are basically slow-cooking the meat ahead of time, then finishing it on the grill.

3 – 4 pounds of chicken pieces (breasts, legs, thighs, or wings with bone and skin)

Georgia Bar-B-Que Sauce
1 ½ cups ketchup
1 cup prepared yellow mustard
1 cup apple cider vinegar
2/3 cup sugar
¼ teaspoon ground (cayenne) red pepper

In a large saucepan that will comfortably hold all the chicken, combine mustard, ketchup and cayenne. Add vinegar and stir. Bring to a boil. Reduce to a simmer and cook 15 to 20 minutes.

Remove 1 cup of sauce from pan and set it aside. Add the chicken pieces to the saucepan. Bring sauce with chicken to a boil, then reduce heat to a low simmer. Simmer the chicken, covered, in the sauce for 20 minutes, stirring occasionally.

Remove chicken from sauce and place on platter. Chicken may be made several hours or even the day ahead up to this point. Cooking sauce may be used to baste chicken on the grill, if desired.

Heat grill until coals turn gray. Grill chicken approximately 10 minutes (about 5 minutes on each side). Baste if necessary, or desired. Serve chicken warm and pass the 1 cup reserved sauce for those who just can't get enough of good bar-b-que.

"Home is where one starts from."
- T. S. Eliot

Ribs on the Barbie with a Green Chili Kick
Serves 4 – 6

The cooking technique and the sauce for this recipe are very similar to the Bar-B-Que Chicken recipe. The big difference is the green chili, which gives the ribs a southwestern flavor.

6 pounds pork spareribs or baby back ribs
3 cups ketchup
2 cups prepared mustard
2 cups apple cider vinegar
1 ⅓ cups sugar
1 cup chopped canned green chilies
½ teaspoon ground (cayenne) red pepper

In a large saucepan, combine ketchup, mustard, vinegar, sugar, chilies and red pepper. Bring to a boil. Reduce heat to low and simmer 15 – 20 minutes. Remove 2 cups of sauce and set aside.

Cut each slab of ribs into thirds, or chunks that will fit comfortably in a stockpot. Place ribs in a pot and pour sauce from the saucepan over them. Bring to a boil, then reduce heat to a simmer. Simmer the ribs, covered, in the sauce for 20 minutes, stirring occasionally.

Remove ribs from sauce and place on platter. Ribs may be made several hours or even the day ahead up to this point. Reserve cooking sauce to baste ribs on the grill.

Heat grill until coals turn gray. Grill ribs 10 – 15 minutes or until done, turning occasionally, and basting with cooking sauce as needed.

Serve ribs warm and pass the sauce that has been set aside.

Fourth of July Dinner

Fourth of July is a time for badminton, croquet, relay races and diving for coins in the swimming pool. It's a time for oohs and ahhs and fireworks. A noisy time of booms and bangs and frightened and delighted children.

It is not a time to spend cooking or cleaning-up in the the kitchen. Dinner should be made ahead so everyone can participate in the games. Clean-up should be minimal because no one wants to miss the fireworks.

With a little work ahead of time, Fourth of July dinner can be a savory treat for everyone and everyone should be able to have fun and enjoy the entertainment.

Dinner Before the Fireworks

Smoked Trout
Boursin with herbs

Spicy Fried Chicken
Corn on the cob

Garden salad with avocado, red onion and
Raspberry Salad Dressing

Red, White and Blueberry Cheesecake
Chocolate Zucchini Cake

Smoked Trout can be purchased at many grocery stores, but is also simple to make yourself in a smoker. It is especially wonderful in that it can be made one to two days in advance, and leftovers make a terrific cocktail spread. The boursin can be made up to a week in advance.

The fried chicken may be prepared the morning of the party or the day before. It is best if served at room temperature.

The cheesecake may be made up to three days in advance. The zucchini cake may be made the morning of the party or several weeks in advance and frozen.

The only last minute preparations should be to boil the corn and toss the salad. The salad bowl and corn pan should be the only pots to wash. Everything else should go in the dishwasher.

Spicy Fried Chicken
Serves 4 – 6

This recipe came from a July 1986 Gourmet Magazine. I made the chicken for a Fourth of July picnic dinner. It has become a tradition in our family and has been made in our house at least once a year ever since. Although I have tried many other fried chicken recipes – this is the one we keep coming back to.

For the marinade:
1 cup plain yogurt
1 cup water
1 tablespoon Tabasco
1 ½ teaspoons salt

4 pounds of chicken – legs, breasts or thighs may be used

For the seasoned flour:
2 cups flour
3 tablespoons sweet paprika
4 teaspoons ground (cayenne) red pepper
2 teaspoons black pepper
2 teaspoons salt
1 teaspoon dried thyme

Use vegetable or canola oil for frying

Make the marinade. In a large bowl whisk together the yogurt, water, Tabasco, and the salt until the mixture is smooth. Add the chicken, tossing to coat. Let the chicken marinate at room temperature for 1 hour or covered and chilled overnight.

Make the seasoned flour. In a shallow bowl stir together the flour, the paprika, the cayenne, the black pepper, salt and thyme.

Working one piece at a time, remove the chicken form the marinade, letting excess drip off, and dredge it in the seasoned flour. Arrange the chicken as it is dredged in a large shallow baking dish sprinkled with some seasoned flour and let it stand, turning and patting on the flour occasionally, for 20 minutes.

In a deep fryer heat oil to 340 degrees, or if using a large heavy skillet – place ½ inch deep oil and heat to 340 degrees. Add as many pieces of chicken as will fit in one layer. Cover and fry chicken for 6 minutes. Turn the chicken and continue to fry, covered, for an additional 6 minutes. Remove lid and fry until golden brown, several more minutes. (If using a deep fryer, 12 minutes at 340 degrees should complete the cooking process.) Legs and thighs my take slightly longer to cook then the breast. Transfer chicken to paper towels and let it drain. Cook remaining chicken in the same manner.

Let the chicken cool completely at room temperature. Chicken may be fried up to 4 hours in advance and kept at room temperature.

"Cooking food, laughing and story telling- that's what we're made of and that's what we enjoy most."
- Ernest Matthew Mickler, American writer

Family Gatherings

Summer is the time for reunions, family get-togethers and large parties. We like to open our homes to friends and family in the summer. We can entertain and serve more people – the doors are open and the porches look so pretty. The grass is in perfect shape for croquet or badminton. The grill smells wonderful and the lawn chairs fall into comfortable circles around the yard.

It's good to have big parties. It's good to see family and friends again.

Hot Summer Salsa and chips (if you want more variety- ask your guests to bring an appetizer)

Pulled Pork
Bar-B-Que Chicken
Georgia Bar-B-Que Sauce
Corn Pudding
Coleslaw
Assorted rolls

Lemon Squash Cake
Watermelon

The pork can be made a day ahead of the party and reheated. The chicken may also be parboiled the day ahead and then grilled at the gathering. The cake may also be baked a day ahead. The salsa and the coleslaw can be made in the morning and served that evening.

Purchase a wide assortment of rolls to be served with dinner. Lots of people like to put their pork on rolls with sauce and eat it like a sandwich. Also make sure there are ample bowls of bar-b-que sauce on the tables.

A "controlled" watermelon seed spitting contest is always good fun after dinner.

Pulled Pork
Serves 10 – 15

When I think of pulled pork, I recall our days in Atlanta when the neighborhood bar-b-que centered around a whole pig being roasted on a spit overnight then "pulled apart" the next day for the feast.

It is not usually possible to roast a whole pig. However, slow-cooking a large roast of pork can provide similar results.

Pulled pork is nothing more than meat which is easily pulled off the bone, shredded, and eaten with a bar-b-que sauce. It may be serve by itself or on a roll. Either way, pulled pork is great party food and an easy way to feed a large crowd.

The pork may be roasted in an oven overnight or cooked all day. The secret to great flavor is long, slow cooking. The pork cooks all by itself, it needs no basting.

9 – 10 pounds pork shoulder or picnic roast

Preheat oven to 300 degrees. In a large roasting pan, place 1 cup water. Salt and pepper pork. Insert slivers of garlic in fat, if desired. Place the pork, fat side up, in roasting pan with water. Cover and bake 5 to 6 hours or until meat begins to fall off bone.

Remove roast from oven. Let cool. Remove visible fat from pork. Pull the pork off the bone and shred it onto a large platter. Pork may be served at room temperature or reheated. The meat may also be moistened with juice from roasting pan, if desired.

Serve pork plain with bar-b-que sauce, or on a roll with sauce.

Corn Pudding
Serves 4

1 15-ounce can of cream style sweet corn
2 eggs
½ cup milk
½ cup sugar
2 tablespoons flour
¼ teaspoon salt

Generously grease a 1½ quart casserole dish. Preheat oven to 450 degrees.

In a medium mixing bowl combine corn, eggs, milk, sugar, flour and salt. Whisk together until combined. If the flour remains a little lumpy, that is fine.

Pour corn mixture into prepared casserole dish. Bake approximately 45 minutes or until set.

"Most people are as happy as they want to be."
- Abe Lincoln

Coleslaw
Serves 6 – 8

1 small head green cabbage
½ small head red cabbage
⅓ cup sugar
⅓ cup cider vinegar
1 teaspoon salt
Freshly grated pepper – to taste

Shred the leaves of the green cabbage. One small head should make about 6 cups of shredded cabbage. Shred the leaves of ½ red cabbage, 2-3 cups.

Place the shredded cabbage in a large serving bowl.

In a small mixing bowl, combine the sugar, vinegar, salt and pepper. Whisk together until sugar is almost dissolved. Pour over shredded cabbage leaves and toss to coat. Refrigerate several hours or until cold.

Whoever though to call cabbages heads?? Why couldn't they just call it cabbage? Or how about a ball of cabbage? Maybe a circle of cabbage? And what about those Cabbage Patch Dolls? Strange.

Vegetable Confetti
Serves 4 – 6

This beautiful vegetable casserole is as delicious as it is colorful. It is a hearty vegetable sidedish. It is sure to impress everyone at potluck dinners, and does wonders to dress-up baked chicken and pork entrees.

It is also a party favorite because it may be made ahead of time.

2 bunches of Swiss chard, or 2 nine-ounce packages of
    frozen chopped spinach
2 red bell peppers, chopped
1 green bell pepper, chopped
1 medium onion, peeled and chopped
2 medium tomatoes
2 tablespoons olive oil
1 cup Monterey Jack Cheese, shredded
½ cup freshly grated Parmesan cheese

Preheat oven to 350 degrees. Grease a 1 or 1½ quart casserole. Rinse chard and remove stems. In a large pot bring about 1 inch of salted water to a boil. Add chard leaves, cover, and blanch for about 2 minutes. Remove leaves, drain, chop, and squeeze them dry. If using spinach, cook according to package directions. Drain and squeeze dry.

In a medium skillet, heat olive oil. Add chopped bell peppers and onions, sauté over medium heat until soft.

Place the cooked, chopped chard in the bottom of the casserole. Top with onion and bell pepper mixture. Slice tomatoes, arrange on top of peppers and onions. Salt and pepper.

Cover tomatoes with shredded Monterey Jack cheese. Top with Parmesan cheese. May be made ahead up to this point. Cover and refrigerate until ready to cook.

Cover casserole and bake for approximately 40 minutes or until bubbly.

If you desire to brown the top, run casserole under broiler before serving.

"Few vegetables look more handsome growing in a kitchen garden than chard."
-   **Alice Waters, <u>Chez Panisse Vegetables</u>**

Farmers' Market Dinner Party

Whether it is going to your local produce stand, the nearby farmers' market, or simply your own backyard garden, August is the month to celebrate vegetables.

One beautiful August weekend our vegetable garden was bursting with glorious produce. I couldn't decide which vegetable to feature at dinner. So I developed this meal that uses as much of the garden bounty as I could pack into four courses.

We served it to just our family of five, but it was so delicious we all agreed it should be used for entertaining.

What a great idea! A Farmers' Market Dinner Party. Invite your guests to come dressed as farmers. Tell them you will be featuring only the finest of the local produce.

Fill a large bowl with colorful vegetables for the centerpiece. Eat outside on the picnic table if the weather and bugs permit.

What could be grander? Fresh food from the local earth, good friends, and family. An evening to remember.

Bruschetta

Cold Zucchini Soup

Grilled Breast of Lamb
Pistouille (eggplant, tomatoes, and peppers)
Roasted Red Potatoes

Carrot Cake

The carrot cake and the zucchini soup may be made the day before the dinner. The pistouille and potatoes may be prepared the morning of the party, and the bruschetta may be assembled several hours before serving. The only last minute preparations are to lightly toast the bread for the bruschetta and grill the lamb.

Grilled Breast of Lamb
Serves 6

Breast of lamb is about half the price of leg of lamb, and if marinated is equally as good.

2 boneless breast of lamb, about 1½ pound each,
Turn end of breasts under and tie with kitchen string, so breast resembles a small roast. You may have the butcher do this for you.

For the Marinade:

½ cup red pepper jelly (jalapeno jelly may be substituted)
½ cup olive oil
2 cloves garlic, minced
Juice of 1 lemon

Combine all marinade ingredients in a bowl or pan large enough to hold the two breasts. Salt and pepper the lamb. Place lamb in marinade and turn to coat. Let stand at room temperature for 1-2 hours or refrigerate overnight.

To grill: lamb should be at room temperature before cooking. When coals turn grey, place lamb on grill and cook covered, turning occasionally. Lamb will take approximately 30 minutes to cook or until meat thermometer registers 140 degrees. Let lamb rest several minutes before carving.

May be served with pepper jelly as a condiment.

Pistouille
Sauteed Eggplant with Tomatoes, Peppers, Garlic and Basil
Serves 4-6

Good hot or cold and leftover, the secret to this dish is reduction of the liquid to intensify the flavor of the vegetables. This recipe is adapted from <u>Mastering the Art of French Cooking,</u> by Julia Child and Simone Beck, Volume Two.

2 pounds eggplant, stem removed, chopped into 1 inch
   cubes
2 pounds fresh tomatoes, peeled, chopped and drained
   (about 2 cups)
4 tablespoons olive oil, divided
1 small onion, minced (about 2/3 cup)
2/3 cup diced yellow bell pepper (if available, otherwise
   green is okay)
2 large cloves garlic, finely minced
12-14 large, fresh basil leaves, minced
3 tablespoons minced fresh parsley

Place chopped eggplant in a colander and sprinkle with salt. Let drain for approximately one hour. While eggplant is macerating in salt, prepare tomatoes.

Peel and chop tomatoes, drain in a colander for approximately 30 minutes.

Next, in a medium to large skillet, cook onion and peppers in 2 tablespoons of olive oil over moderate heat until tender and translucent, but not brown; about 10 minutes. Add chopped and drained tomatoes. Cover pan and simmer for five minutes. Uncover pan and simmer for an additional five minutes, or until juices have almost entirely evaporated. Remove from heat and set aside.

Rinse eggplant and pat dry. Place remaining 2 tablespoons of olive oil in a skillet and heat. Add eggplant and sauté until golden brown. Drain on a paper towel.

Add cooked eggplant to tomato mixture and simmer uncovered for about 10 minutes to blend flavors and evaporate more liquid. Mixture should form a thick mass.

In a separate bowl, mash together the basil and garlic to form a paste. Fold into hot eggplant.

May be made ahead of time up to this point. Just before serving fold in parsley.

May be served hot, at room temperature, or cold.

"It's better to buy local foods that haven't traveled 1,500 miles to get here. It's healthier for our planet and for our bodies."
- Morgan Rafferty, California Central Coast Grown board member, February, 2008

Roasted Red Potatoes
Serves 6

These potatoes are a mainstay of our family in the summer. They're better than French Fries and perfect for entertaining because they can be made hours in advance. Try them with grilled steak, hamburgers, chicken, or fish.

3 pounds red potatoes, leave the skin on and cut into bite-
    sized wedges, about 1½ inches long
2 tablespoons olive oil
1 tablespoon chopped garlic
1 teaspoon Kosher salt

Preheat oven to 400 degrees. Place potatoes on a baking sheet, skin side up. Prick potatoes with a fork. Bake 25 minutes or until potatoes are easily pierced with a fork or knife.

In a glass bowl large enough to hold potatoes, place oil, garlic and salt. Stir. Remove potatoes from baking sheet and place in bowl. Toss to coat.

Potatoes may be served immediately. However, I think they are better if they are left to stand at room temperature for several hours. This enables the flavors of the oil, garlic, and salt to infuse the potatoes.

What is Success?

What is Success?
To laugh often and much;
To win the respect of intelligent people
And the affection of children;
To earn the appreciation of honest critics
And endure the betrayal of false friends;
To appreciate beauty;
To find the best in others;
To leave the world a bit better, whether by
A healthy child, a garden patch,
Or a redeemed social condition;
To know even one life has breathed
easier because you have lived;
This is to have succeeded.
-Ralph Waldo Emerson

Red Potato Salad with Dill
Serves 6-8

Great picnic food; this side dish is delicious with fried chicken and all grilled food.

3 pounds red potatoes, cleaned, leaving skin on, halved if
    large
1½ cups chopped celery
1 cup red onion, chopped
1 cup mayonnaise
1 cup sour cream
1 tablespoon chopped fresh parsley leaves
1½ teaspoons chopped fresh dill leaves (or ½ teaspoon
    dried dill leaves)
1 teaspoon salt
Dash Tabasco, or to taste
Freshly ground pepper to taste

Bring a large pot of salted water to a boil. Add potatoes and continue to boil until potatoes may be easily pierced with a fork; about 20 minutes. Drain potatoes.

In a large bowl, place chopped celery, onion, mayonnaise, sour cream, parsley, dill, salt, pepper, and Tabasco. Stir to combine. When potatoes have cooled, cut into bite sized pieces and stir into mixture. Refrigerate several hours before serving.

Potato salad will keep in the refrigerator for several days. However, the dill flavor will intensify the longer the salad is refrigerated.

Two Bean Salad
Or
Two Bean Salsa
Or
Two Bean Relish
Serves 6

1 15-ounce can black beans, drained
1 15-ounce can white beans, drained
½ red bell pepper, cut into ¼ inch dice
½ green bell pepper, cut into ¼ inch dice
½ cup diced red onion
2 jalapeno peppers, seeds removed, finely diced
Juice of 1 lime
⅓ cup chopped fresh cilantro or parsley
¼ teaspoon ground cumin
1 teaspoon salt
Ground black pepper to taste
1-2 tablespoons olive oil, optional

Combine all ingredients in a large bowl. Mix well and refrigerate at least several hours to let flavors blend. May be made one day in advance. Especially good with grilled chicken or pork.

Is it a Salad, a Salsa, or a Relish???
Definitions according to Random House Dictionary:
Salad n. 1. a dish, usually served cold, consisting of vegetables, such as lettuce, tomatoes, etc, or of fruit meat, seafood, or eggs, mixed with a dressing.
Salsa n. 1. a form of Latin American dance music with exciting rhythms. 2. sauce, esp. chili sauce.
Relish n. 1. liking or enjoyment of the taste of something. 2. pleasurable appreciation or liking or anything. 3. something savory or appetizing, as a sweet pickle or minced vegetables.

Coriander or Cilantro

Coriander, sometimes called Chinese parsley, is often given its Mexican name, cilantro, in the United States. The leaves should be added at the end of cooking or sprinkled over a dish before it is served, as its flavor dissipates when heated. Coriander seed is often used as a pickling spice and in marinades and court-bouillons.

Cool Dinner for a Hot Summer Night

A cool soup, a hearty salad, and a cold berry pie is a welcome menu for any hot August night. The soup and the pie are easily prepared earlier in the day and have friends or family help assemble the salad at the last minute.

Gazpacho

Fillet of Beef Salad
with
Blue Cheese Dressing and Sesame Seeds
Garlic Bread

Mom's Strawberry Pie

"Summer time and the living is easy. Fish are jumping and the cotton is high."
- **Porgy and Bess**

Fillet of Beef Salad
With
Blue Cheese Dressing and Sesame Seeds
Serves 4

This is a wonderful summer salad dinner. It is also a great way to use left-over fillet mignon, sirloin, or roast beef.

1 pound beef, such as sirloin, or London Broil, sliced thin, cut into ½ inch wide strips
3 ounces blue cheese
2 tablespoons hot water
⅓ cup mayonnaise
⅓ cup sour cream
¼ teaspoon Tabasco
8 cups mixed salad greens, cleaned, dried, and torn into bite-sized pieces
2 tablespoons Asian sesame oil
2 medium carrots, cut into thin sticks (julienne)
1 tablespoon rice vinegar
1 medium tomato, cut into ⅓ inch dice

To make the Dressing:
Place the cheese in a small bowl. Break apart with a fork, add hot water and stir until nearly smooth. Stir in mayonnaise, sour cream, Tabasco, and freshly ground pepper to taste. The dressing may be made ahead and refrigerated up to 5 days ahead.

To make the Beef:
In a large skillet, heat the sesame oil until nearly smoking. Add half of the beef to the pan in a single layer. Sprinkle with salt and pepper and sear over moderately high heat, turning once, until browned. Transfer to a plate and cover to keep warm. Repeat with remaining beef.

To make the Salad:

Remove the skillet from heat and add carrots and white sesame seeds. Stir in vinegar. Place salad greens in a mixing bowl. Pour carrot mixture over greens and toss. Season with salt and pepper.

Mound salad onto four dinner-sized plates. Arrange ¼ of warm beef on each. Top with diced tomato. Spoon approximately 2 tablespoons of blue cheese dressing over each salad. Serve immediately, passing the remaining dressing separately.

Grilled Chicken Niçoise
Serves 4-5

An interesting twist to an old classic. Canned tuna may be substituted for grilled chicken to create Salad Niçoise.

4 boneless, skinless chicken breasts, about 2 pounds
Olive oil and lemon juice
1 pound green beans, ends trimmed
4 medium red potatoes, halved or quartered
4 hard boiled eggs, quartered
1 pint cherry tomatoes
2 tablespoons fresh chopped basil

Dressing:
6 tablespoons vegetable oil
6 tablespoons olive oil
2 tablespoons wine vinegar
2 teaspoons Dijon mustard
2 cloves garlic, minced
1½ teaspoons salt
½ teaspoon sugar
1 teaspoon chopped fresh thyme leaves or ½ teaspoon dried
    thyme

In a pint sized jar with a tight-fitting lid, combine all dressing ingredients. Shake well until blended. Set aside.

Pound chicken breasts until 1/4 -⅓ inch thick. Rub with olive oil and lemon juice. Set aside.

Bring a large pot of water to a boil. Boil green beans until just tender. Remove and place in a bowl of ice water. When cool, remove beans and place in refrigerator.

In the same boiling water, place potatoes. Boil until tender. Remove and place in bowl of ice water. When cool, remove potatoes and place in refrigerator.

Salt and pepper chicken breasts. Grill or sauté breasts until golden brown on both sides and cooked through.

On each serving plate, arrange a portion of chicken, green beans, potatoes, tomatoes, and hard boiled eggs. Sprinkle basil over serving plates. Drizzle dressing over vegetables and meat.

"Live in each season as it passes. Breathe the air. Drink the drink. Taste the fruit"
- Henry David Thoreau

Summer III

Desserts

Nectarine and Peach Crisp
Serves 6

Nothing is simpler or more delicious than a freshly baked crisp. Substitute other fruits if you desire. Serve warm or cold, with or without ice cream or whipped cream.

2 cups sliced nectarines, skin on
2 cups peeled and sliced peaches
¼ cup brown sugar
1 cup flour
¾ cup sugar
½ teaspoon cinnamon
8 tablespoons butter (1 stick)

Preheat oven to 350 degrees. Grease a cake pan or an 8x8-inch baking dish. In a medium bowl place nectarines and peaches. Add brown sugar and toss to coat. Set aside.

In a small bow, mix the flour, sugar, and cinnamon. Cut in butter. Using a pastry blender or two knives, cut butter into the flour mixture until it resembles small peas.

Place nectarines and peaches in baking dish. Pour flour mixture over top. Bake 30 minutes or until fruit is bubbling and the topping begins to brown.

Enjoy life. Take time to relax. Don't feel guilty. Life is too short and full of too many wonderful pleasures. Don't miss out on the good stuff.

"I'm beginning to trust that the gods are not going to snatch my firstborn if I happen to enjoy my life."
- **Frances Mayes, Under the Tuscan Sun**

Single Layer Chocolate Zucchini Cake
Serves 12

The zucchini adds nutritional value to this rich cake, but its real asset is that it keeps the cake extra moist. Even those who swear they hate zucchini will love this chocolate delicacy.

Cake:
2 cups grated, unpeeled zucchini (2-3 small zucchini)
2¼ cups flour
½ cup unsweetened cocoa
1 teaspoon baking soda
1 teaspoon salt
1¾ cups sugar
½ cup butter
½ cup vegetable oil
2 eggs
1 teaspoon vanilla extract
½ cup plain, low-fat yogurt

Chocolate Frosting:
1 cup whipping cream
2 cups semisweet chocolate chips
2 tablespoons light corn syrup

For Cake:
Preheat oven to 325 degrees. Butter and flour a 13x9x2-inch baking pan. Sift flour, cocoa powder, baking soda, and salt into a medium bowl. Beat sugar, butter, and oil in a large bowl until well blended. Add eggs one at a time, beating well after each addition. Beat in vanilla extract and yogurt. Mix in dry ingredients. Mix in grated zucchini. Pour batter into prepared baking pan. Bake until cake tester inserted into center comes out clean, about 45 minutes. Cool cake before frosting.

For Frosting:

Scald whipping cream in heavy medium saucepan over medium heat. Remove from heat. Add chocolate pieces and stir until melted and smooth. Mix in light corn syrup. Transfer to a medium bowl. Refrigerate frosting until just spreadable, about 15 minutes. Once frosted, refrigerate the cake until ready to serve.

Cake may be prepared one day ahead, or it may be frozen

"There is no job harder than being a wife and a mother. It's a position that should be respected and honored, not looked upon as some sappy alternative."
-Patti Smith, influential poet and musician of the 1970's

Red, White, and Blueberry Cheesecake
Serves 8-10

Similar to a New York style cheesecake, this shallow cheesecake is delicious with a variety of toppings, or it excellent plain. Try glazing the cake with sour cream instead of jam. Or top the cake with an assortment of fresh summer berries. Grated chocolate is also a delicious topping.

Cake:
20 ounces cream cheese
1 cup sugar
2 teaspoons grated lemon peel
¼ teaspoon vanilla
3 eggs

Topping:
⅓ cup strawberry jam
½ cup blueberries

Preheat oven to 300 degrees. Grease an 8-inch springfoam pan.

Beat cream cheese in a large mixing bowl. Gradually add sugar and continue to beat until fluffy.

Add lemon peel and vanilla. Beat in eggs, one at a time, mixing well after each addition. Pour mixture into prepared springfoam pan.

Bake one hour or until done. The cheesecake is done when the edges pull away from the sides and cracks begin to form in the center of the cake.

Cool on a rack. Remove the sides of the springfoam pan. Cake may be made up to 3 days ahead at this point. Cover and refrigerate. When ready to serve add topping. Heat jam to make it spreadable. Glaze the top of the cake with jam. Place blueberries on top of jam. Refrigerate cake until ready to serve.

Carrot Cake
Serves 10-12

Cake:

3 cups peeled and grated carrots

2 cups water

1½ cup vegetable oil

4 eggs, beaten

2 cups flour

1 teaspoon salt

2 teaspoons baking soda

2 teaspoons cinnamon

Cream Cheese Icing:

8 tablespoons butter, room temperature

1 8-ounce package cream cheese, room temperature

1 1-pound box confectioners' sugar

2 teaspoons vanilla

½ cup chopped pecans

For Cake:

Preheat oven to 350 degrees. Butter a 10-inch tube pan or springfoam pan.

In a medium mixing bowl, combing sugar, oil, and beaten eggs. Sift flour, salt, soda, and cinnamon together. Add flour mixture to egg mixture. Fold in carrots.

Pour mixture into buttered pan and bake about 50 minutes or until a cake tester inserted into the center comes out clean. Let cool before icing.

For Cream Cheese Icing:

Cream butter and cream cheese. Add sugar and vanilla, beat well. Stir in nuts. Ice cake.

Keep in refrigerator. May be made a day ahead. Freezes well.

Meringue Cookies
Makes 6-8, 3-4 inch cookies

4-6 egg whites (1/2 cup), room temperature
Pinch of salt
1 cup sugar
1 teaspoon vanilla

Place egg whites and salt in a medium mixing bowl. Beat until frothy, then increase speed and beat until peaks form. Gradually add sugar one tablespoon at a time until all in incorporated and the mixture is stiff and shiny. Beat in vanilla. Do not over-beat the egg whites or they will lose their volume and turn to syrup. To bake, use either Baking Technique 1 or Baking Technique 2.

Baking Technique 1:
Preheat oven to 250 degrees. Place brown paper or parchment paper on a baking sheet. Drop meringues by large tablespoons onto baking sheet. Place in oven, close door and turn the oven off. Let the meringues sit in the oven overnight.

Baking Technique 2:
Preheat oven to 250 degrees. Prepare baking sheets as in Technique 1. Place meringues in oven and bake for one hour.

The ideal texture of a meringue is crunchy on the outside with a touch of stickiness on the inside.

Storage:
Wrap tightly in plastic wrap once they have cooled. Store up to three days or freeze.

Meringue Cookies with Peaches and Berries
Serves 6

Meringue Cookies
Six ripe peaches
1 cup fresh berries
1 cup whipping cream

Follow recipe for Meringue Cookies. Figure one cookie per serving. Allow one peach per serving. Use whatever small berries are in season: strawberries, blueberries, blackberries, and raspberries all work well.

Whip the cream with a little sugar (about 1 tablespoon) until the cream holds soft peaks. Keep refrigerated until ready for use.

Peel the peaches and remove the pit. Slice one peach on each serving plate. Top the peach with a meringue cookie. Place several dollops of whipped cream around plate. Garnish the cream with berries. Serve immediately.

How to Whip Cream:

Cream should always be chilled before whipping. It is also advantageous, if you have the time and if you remember, to chill the bowl. Whisk the cold cream with an electric beater until it forms stiff peaks. If over-whisked, cream will turn to butter. This is a wonderful experiment, or teaching tool, for young children. However, when you are having a dinner party, it is important to remember that most people want whipped cream on their dessert, not butter. Consequently, it is wiser to pay attention to the whipping process.

Heavy cream and whipping cream can be whipped to about double their volume and will stay stiff for several hours.

Lemon Squash Cake
With
Lemon Frosting
Serves 8-10

This extra lemony, moist cake is a perfect summer dessert. It also goes well with tea or coffee. Try garnishing it with yellow nasturtium flowers or blue pansies.

Cake:
2 cups grated, unpeeled yellow crookneck squash (about 1 pound)
2¼ cup flour
1 teaspoon baking soda
1 teaspoon salt
1½ cups sugar
½ cup butter (1 stick), softened
½ cup vegetable oil
2 eggs
1 teaspoon lemon extract
1 tablespoon freshly grated lemon peel
½ cup sour cream

Frosting:
2 cups confectioners' sugar
¼ cup butter (4 tablespoons), softened
1 or more tablespoon cream (or milk)
Juice of 1 lemon

For Cake:
Preheat oven to 325 degrees. Butter and flour two 8-inch cake pans. Sift flour, baking soda, and salt into a medium bowl. Beat sugar, butter, and oil in a large bowl until well blended. Add eggs one at a time, beating well after each addition. Beat in lemon extract, lemon peel, and sour cream. Mix in dry ingredients. Add squash and stir until blended. Pour batter into prepared cake pans. Bake

cake until cake tester inserted into the center comes out clean, about 50 minutes. Cool cake on rack before removing from pan. Frost.

For Lemon Frosting:
Blend the butter and confectioners' sugar well. While beating add cream until desired spreading consistency is achieved. Stir in lemon juice.

Cake may be prepared one day in advance. Keep refrigerated. The cake may also be frozen.

"Certainly, food is not the only way to show love, but it is one of the pleasantest and simplest."
- **Barbara Kafka, American Writer**

Mom's Strawberry Pie
Serves 6

1 baked 9-inch pie crust in pan (p.145)

1 pound strawberries (about 1 quart), divided
1 cup sugar
½ cup water
2 tablespoons cornstarch

If pie crust has not already been baked, do so and set it aside.
To bake an unfilled pie crust:
Preheat oven to 425 degrees. Prick pie shell all over with a fork. Bake pie shell for approximately 12 minutes, or until the edges begin to brown. Remove to rack to cool.

For Strawberry Pie:
Clean and slice 2 cups of strawberries. Set remaining berries aside for use in finished pie.
Place the 2 cups of sliced strawberries in a medium saucepan. Stir in sugar and cook over a medium-high heat until mixture boils. Continue to cook and stir for about 5 minutes.
While strawberries are cooking, dissolve cornstarch in the ¼ cup of water.
After 5 minutes of cooking, slowly add cornstarch to boiling berries, stirring constantly. Continue to cook for another minute or until the mixture thickens.
Pour cooked berries into baked pie crust. Clean remaining berries. Cut in halves or quarters and randomly stick into the pie. Refrigerate the pie until cool. Serve cold. A dollop of whipped cream or vanilla ice cream is very good with this summer dessert.

Butterscotch Brownies
Serves 15 or more

2 cups light brown sugar
2/3 cup butter
3 eggs
1¼ cups flour
2 tablespoons baking powder
2 tablespoons vanilla
¼ cup sour cream
1 cup (about 6 ounces) butterscotch chips

Preheat oven to 350 degrees. Grease a 9x13 inch baking pan. In a medium saucepan, place the sugar and butter. Cook over low heat, stirring occasionally, until butter is melted and mixture is smooth. Cool. Beat the 3 eggs into butter/sugar mixture.

In a large mixing bowl, sift the flour and baking powder. Add butter mixture to flour and stir. Mix in vanilla, sour cream, and butterscotch chips. Pour into baking pan. Bake 25 minutes, or until cake tester inserted into the center comes out clean. Try not to over bake.

Fall

Fall, the glorious season we all wait for – wait for- and wait for. Long tired of salads and grilled foods, we wait for the weather to change so we may come inside, turn on the oven and make an apple pie – create a meat loaf – or cook-up our first batch of homemade soup.

We wait when the children go back to school and the temperature is still ninety degrees. We wait while the summer flowers get mildew and the chrysanthemums start to bloom. We wait while the pumpkins rot on our front door step.

But then it happens – that cold rainy day – the chill in the air and the first fire of the season. The kitchen calls us. We don a sweater and create a wonderful soul-warming meal that all enjoy.

The leaves change colors. Our foods are full of reds and yellows. The brussel sprouts taste better than ever and we can't get enough apples.

But hurry –for soon the snow will come and winter winds will blow away the color and warmth of fall.

Fall I

Appetizers

Soups

Salads

Breads

Breakfast Foods

Tailgate Party

Tailgate parties can be very formal or very casual. My son's idea of a good tailgate is to pack up the grill, fill the cooler with drinks, hot dogs and hamburgers. Grab a bag of chips. Don't forget the condiments, - and you're off to the football game.

I, on the other hand, like warm soup from a thermos. A first course of green tomato and mozzarella tart with roasted red bell pepper sauce. Baked chicken with fresh herbs presented on a silver platter. Grandma's china. Tossed green salad. And for dessert – those lovely little finger pastries from my favorite bakery.

It doesn't really matter what or how you eat at a Tailgate Party – the purpose is to get together with good friends, share food, and root for the home team. How can one not have a good time?

Green Tomato and Mozzarella Tart
With Roasted Red Bell Pepper Sauce
Serves 6

This is a great first course for dinner parties, excellent for brunch with grilled sausage – and delicious as a lunch for light dinner entrée.

For the Tart

Pastry for 1, 9-inch pie crust(p.145)
3 medium green tomatoes (about 1 lb.), sliced into ½ inch
    thick circles
2 medium onions, sliced thin
½ tablespoon butter
1 tablespoon olive oil
½ pound mozzarella cheese, shredded
1 heaping teaspoon fresh thyme leaves
salt and pepper to taste

Preheat oven to 375 degrees. Roll out the pie crust and pat into a 9-inch quiche pan or pie pan. In a large skillet, melt butter and olive oil. Add onions and sauté over low heat (covered and stirring occasionally) until onions are soft and just starting to brown, about 15 minutes.

Spread onions over the pie crust. Top with cheese and place tomatoes in a single layer over the mozzarella. Sprinkle tart with thyme, salt and pepper.

Bake for 1 hour.

When tart is finished baking, let cool on a pie rack for several minutes before slicing. Slice into six pieces. Serve on a plate drizzled with Roasted Red Bell Pepper Sauce.

Roasted Red Bell Pepper Sauce
Makes about ½ cup

This sauce is heavenly with the Green Tomato and Mozzarella Tart, but it is also wonderful with crab cakes.

1 large red bell pepper
2 tablespoons minced shallots
½ cup white wine
2 tablespoons white wine vinegar
½ cup (1 stick) butter

To roast bell pepper, place pepper over burner on gas stove or under a broiler. Roast until the entire pepper is charred – turning as necessary to ensure all sides are blackened. Place roasted pepper in a paper bag to steam for several minutes. Remove charred skin and seeds. Puree pepper. Place ⅓ cup pepper puree aside for use in sauce. Reserve any remaining puree for another use.

In a small sauce pan, bring shallots, wine and vinegar to a boil. Continue to boil until mixture is reduced to 1 tablespoon. Strain liquid into a quart size pan, add the ⅓ cup pepper puree.

Over medium heat, add butter, one tablespoon at a time, whisking continually. When all of the butter is incorporated into the sauce, remove from heat and serve.

Pie Crust
Pastry for two 9-inch pie shells

Homemade pie crust can make a difference between a good pie and a great pie. This recipe is adapted from The Fannie Farmer Cookbook.

1 ¾ cups flour
1 teaspoon salt
2/3 cup cold butter
⅓ cup ice water

In a medium mixing bowl place the flour and salt. Cut in the butter. Mix with a pastry blender until mixture is in even bits, about the size of peas. Sprinkle the water over the flour by tablespoons, stirring with a fork. Enough water has been added when you can pat the dough into a ball. (more or less water may be needed, depending upon the flour)

Divide pastry into two balls. Each will make a single, 9-inch pie shell. Wrap the dough in wax paper or plastic wrap and chill until ready for use. Dough should chill at least one hour before serving. Dough will keep several days in the refrigerator or may be frozen.

"The Cocktail Hour"

Never plan more than one hour for cocktails before a dinner party. Forty-five minutes seems to be perfect.

The purpose of "cocktails" is to provide a time of greeting, sharing and relaxing.

A too-long cocktail hour can ruin appetites and the best planned dinner party. A too-short, or lack of "cocktail time", can make guests feel rushed and hurried to bring the evening to an end.

Marinated Shrimp and Vegetables
Serves 6 – 8

This is a wonderful appetizer recipe. It is one of my favorites because it may be prepared up to a week in advance, and must be made at least 48 hours in advance. It has a little something for everyone, and is great any time of the year.

1 cup vegetable oil
1 cup cider vinegar
Juice of 3 lemons
5 bay leaves
1 teaspoon dill seed
1 teaspoon celery salt
Dash ground cayenne pepper
2 tablespoons sugar
1 teaspoon crushed whole peppercorns
½ teaspoon dried tarragon leaves
1 teaspoon dry mustard
1½ pound shrimp, cleaned and cooked
3 medium onions, sliced
1 14-ounce can artichoke hearts in water, drained
1 14-ounce can black olives, drained
½ pound small fresh mushrooms, sliced in half if large.
    Canned mushrooms, drained are also OK.

In a medium saucepan, combine all ingredients except shrimp and vegetables. Bring mixture to a boil. Reduce heat and simmer for 10 minutes. Add shrimp and simmer 3 additional minutes.

Choose a large casserole with lid. Place a layer of sliced onion on bottom, then a layer of shrimp. Repeat until all onion and shrimp is used. Cover shrimp and onions with hot marinade. When cool, cover casserole and refrigerate at least 48 hours and up to one week.

At least 2 hours before serving, and not more than 24 hours; mix artichokes, olives and mushrooms into shrimp and onion casserole. Refrigerate until ready to serve. Serve with cocktail picks or toothpicks.

"T'is an ill cook that cannot lick his own fingers."
-William Shakespeare

Butternut Squash Soup with Sorrel and Curry Puree with Pumpkin Seed Garnish

Serves 6

This elegant yet simple soup is as beautiful to look at as it is delicious to taste. Garnished with toasted pumpkin seeds it is a prefect fall soup. The tart, green taste of the sorrel is a perfect compliment to the sweet butternut squash.

Sorrel is a wonderful leafy green. It develops its best flavor in cool weather. Although it is easy to grow in the home garden, it is not always available at the supermarket. If you can not find sorrel, spinach may be substituted.

Butternut Soup

1 tablespoon butter
2 tablespoons olive oil
1 medium onion, chopped
1 large shallot, finely chopped, about 2 tablespoons
1 large butternut squash, about 1 ½ pounds, peeled, seeded and coarsely chopped
4 cups chicken stock

In a large sauce pan, heat oil and butter. Add onions, shallots and squash – sauté over medium heat until onions are soft. Add stock, bring mixture to a boil. Reduce heat to low and simmer until squash is soft and breaks apart with a spoon, about 30 minutes. In a food processor or blender, puree soup in batches. Return to saucepan. Add salt and pepper to taste.

Sorrel and Curry Puree

1 bunch sorrel, 8 – 10 ounces, rinsed, stems removed
½ cup water
¼ teaspoon mild curry powder

In a small saucepan, bring water to boil. Add sorrel and boil until cooked, about 2 minutes. Sorrel will turn a brownish-green color. In a blender or food processor, puree sorrel mixture with curry. Place puree in a squeeze bottle (an empty mustard bottle works well). If a squeeze bottle is not available, place puree in a small bowl and use a spoon to dribble onto soup.

Toasted Pumpkin Seeds

1 cup pumpkin seeds

Preheat oven to 350 degrees. If using fresh pumpkin seeds, make sure they have been rinsed well and dried on a paper towel.

Place pumpkin seeds on a cookie sheet. Sprinkle with vegetable oil and salt. Stir to coat. Bake 15 – 20 minutes or until brown and crisp – stir occasionally.

These toasted seeds are also delicious to eat like nuts.

Assembly

Ladle hot soup into bowls. Dribble puree in a large circle on the soup. Place several toasted pumpkin seeds in the center. Serve

Options

Although this soup is magnificent prepared in the above manner, it may be served many other ways and is equally good. The pumpkin seeds are optional – although their salty crunch adds a nice dimension.

The butternut soup is very good by itself. It may be prepared 24 hours in advance or may be made ahead, frozen and reheated.

Leave out the sorrel. The curry powder may be added directly to the soup – more or less may be added, depending upon your taste.

New England Clam Chowder
Serves 12

This is one of my children's favorite soups. It makes a lot but it is delicious left-over. It is also one of my favorite lunches.

¼ pound of bacon diced and blanched in boiling water
2 cups chopped celery (about 6 stalks)
2 tablespoons olive oil
2 medium onions, peeled and chopped
1 quart chicken stock
1 heaping teaspoon fresh thyme leaves, chopped – or ½ teaspoon dried thyme
1 ½ pound potatoes peeled and diced
8 tablespoons butter (1 stick)
6 tablespoons flour
1 quart milk
Three, 6.5 ounce cans of minced clams with liquid (about 2 cups)

In a small saucepan, bring water and the diced bacon to a boil. Blanch for 2 minutes. Remove bacon and let drain on a paper towel.

In a large stock pot, heat oil over medium heat. Add chopped celery and onions and sauté until soft. Stir in stock. Add bacon, thyme and diced potatoes (if using red potatoes I like to leave the skin on for color in the soup). Bring mixture to a simmer and continue to cook until potatoes are soft.

While the stock is simmering, melt the 8 tablespoons of butter in a medium saucepan. Add the flour and stir until mixture foams. Slowly add milk and continue to stir. Continue to stir over medium heat until mixture thickens.

When potatoes are soft, add thickened milk to stock. Bring to a simmer and add clams with their liquid. Add salt and pepper to taste. Serve warm.

Cauliflower and Arugula Soup
Serves 6

This is a delicious, unusual, and very pretty soup.

1 small head of cauliflower (1 ¼ - 1 ½ pounds)
4 cups water
1 heaping teaspoon salt
2 cups packed arugula, stems removed
4 tablespoons butter
¼ cup minced shallots
3 tablespoons flour
3 cups milk

Remove and discard outer leaves and stem of cauliflower. Break cauliflower head into florets. In a medium saucepan bring 4 cups of water and salt to a boil. Drop florets into water and continue to boil for 2 minutes. Remove cauliflower from water, set aside in a bowl. Measure out 3 cups of the water used to boil cauliflower, this will be used with the milk to make the soup.

Clean arugula. Remove stems and pack in a 2 cup measurer. Set aside.

In a large saucepan or pot, melt butter. Add shallots and sauté over medium heat until soft. Stir in flour and cook for an additional minute or two. Whisk in milk and boiled cauliflower water, continue to stir until mixture comes to a boil. Reduce heat to a simmer. Add cauliflower and cook until soft, about 15 minutes. Stir occasionally. Stir in arugula and cook an additional 10 minutes. Puree. Season with salt and pepper to taste. When ready to serve, reheat soup.

Arugula

Arugula is a lettuce that is similar in taste to dandelion leaves. Also known as rocket, it has a bitter-peppery taste. Use the small, younger leaves for a mild flavor and remove tough stems. Use arugula in mixed green salads. Try growing it in your garden. It grows better and faster than most weeds in my garden.

Traditional Caesar Salad
Serves 8

On one of the first dates with my future husband, I made this salad. He soon started coming over for dinner every night and requesting my Caesar salad. He probably would not have asked me to marry him, if not for this recipe.

½ cup olive oil
2 teaspoons Worcestershire sauce
2 teaspoons garlic salt
2 eggs
Juice of 1 lemon (about 2 tablespoons fresh lemon juice)
2 heads romaine lettuce, (or enough for 8 servings)
2/3 cups grated Parmesan cheese, about 3 ounces
Croutons, if desired
Anchovies, if desired

In a large salad bowl place oil, Worcestershire sauce, garlic salt, eggs and lemon juice. Whisk together. Tear romaine leaves into bite-size pieces. Add lettuce, Parmesan cheese and croutons, if desired. Toss to coat. Season with freshly grated pepper. Place anchovies on top of salad, if using.

A Caesar salad becomes a meal in itself when sauté chicken or shrimp are added.

Caesar Salad Sans Egg
Serves 8

This is a great recipe for anyone who is leery of using raw eggs in their salad dressing.

½ cup olive oil
2 tablespoons red wine vinegar
Juice of 1 lemon (about 2 tablespoons fresh lemon juice)
1 tablespoon Worcestershire sauce
1 teaspoon Dijon mustard
1 large garlic clove, minced
Several drops Tabasco
2 heads romaine lettuce (or enough for 8 servings)
2/3 cup freshly grated Parmesan cheese (about 3 ounces)
Croutons, if desired
Anchovies, if desired

Whisk olive oil, vinegar, lemon juice, Worcestershire, mustard, garlic and Tabasco in a small bowl. Tear lettuce leaves into bite-size pieces. Place lettuce in salad bowl; add cheese, dressing and crouton, if desired. Toss to coat. Season with freshly ground pepper.
Place anchovies on top of salad, if using.

Herb Croutons
Makes 1 cup croutons

These tasty croutons dress-up any salad. They are particularly good in a Caesar salad. The recipe is easily doubled.

1 cup bread cubes, day-old bread cut into bite-size cubes
2 tablespoons butter
Dash herb seasoning
Dash seasoned salt
Dash garlic salt

Preheat oven to 300 degree. Bake bread cubes until brown, about 10 minutes. In a small skillet, melt butter, add seasonings, add croutons and sauté until well coated. Toss in salad.

Garlic Croutons

Croutons may also be made by tossing 1 cup toasted bread cubes in ⅓ cup olive oil and 1 clove of garlic, minced. Let the bread cubes steep in the garlic/oil for at least one hour before serving.

Banana Bread
Makes 2 loaves

While developing this banana bread recipe, I felt very strongly that not only should the bread be moist and tasty – but the recipe should provide two loaves, one to give away and one to keep.

So on a dismal fall day when the overripe bananas are starting to attract fruit flies, make some bread. Give a loaf to a neighbor or a friend or co-worker, and savor the other loaf for yourself.

1½ cup mashed ripe bananas (3 – 5 bananas)
½ pound butter (2 sticks), softened
2 cups sugar
4 eggs
4 cups flour
1½ teaspoon salt
1 teaspoon baking soda
2 teaspoons vanilla extract
1 large, slightly under-ripe banana, sliced

Preheat oven to 325 degrees. Grease two 9x5x3 inch bread pans. In a small bowl, mash ripe bananas. Set aside.

In a large mixing bowl, cream together butter and sugar until light and fluffy. Beat in eggs.

In another bowl, sift together flour, salt and baking soda. Mix together flour mixture with egg-butter mixture. Stir in mashed bananas, vanilla and sliced banana. Stir to combine. Divide mixture evenly between bread pans.

Bake 60 – 75 minutes or until done. Turn bread out onto a rack to cool. Freezes well.

For variation, add 2/3 cup chopped walnuts to dough.

My mother used to say, 'the older you get, the better you get ... unless you're a banana."
- Rose Nylund, <u>Chicken Soup for the Teenage Soul II</u>

Cranberry Nut Bread
Makes 2 Large Loaves

This attractive and delicious bread is perfect for breakfast the morning after Thanksgiving. Make the bread weeks, or even a month, in advance and freeze. No one feels like cooking the morning after Thanksgiving, but the family will still be hungry. (Just don't forget to take the bread out of the freezer the night before.) Cranberry bread and some fresh fruit make a delightful breakfast.

This bread is also lovely to have as a gift during the holiday season.

1 12-ounce package cranberries, rinsed and picked over
¾ cup butter (1½ sticks), softened
2 cups sugar
3 eggs
2 teaspoons vanilla extract
4 cups flour
2 teaspoons baking powder
2 teaspoons cinnamon
1 teaspoon salt
¼ teaspoon ground nutmeg
¼ teaspoon allspice
2/3 cup sour cream
½ cup chopped pecans

Preheat oven to 350 degrees. Grease two 9x5x3 inch bread pans. Steam the cranberries for 2-3 minutes or until the skin starts to split. Set aside.

In a medium mixing bowl, cream together the softened butter and sugar. Add eggs and beat until combined. Beat in vanilla.

In a large bowl sift together flour, baking powder, cinnamon, salt, nutmeg, and allspice. Stir egg mixture into flour mixture. Stir in sour cream. Add cranberries and nuts. Stir to combine. Divide dough between the two loaf pans.

Bake for 1 hour or until done. The bread is done when a tester inserted into the center comes out clean.
Freezes well.

'Let not your life be wholly without an object, though it be only to ascertain the flavor of a cranberry, for it will not be only the quality of an insignificant berry that you will have tasted, but the flavor of your life to that extent, and it will be such a sauce as no wealth can buy."
- <u>Wild Fruits</u> by Henry David Thoreau

Apple-Cinnamon Coffee Cake
Serves 8-10

Cake:
1½ cup sugar
4 tablespoons butter (1/2 stick)
1 teaspoon vanilla extract
8 ounces cream cheese, softened
2 eggs
1½ cups flour
1½ teaspoons baking powder
½ teaspoon salt
3 cups peeled and chopped apples (about 3 apples)

Topping:
¼ cup sugar
2 teaspoons cinnamon

Preheat oven to 350 degrees. Grease an 8 inch springform pan.

In a medium mixing bowl, cream together butter, cream cheese, and vanilla. Beat until light and fluffy. Add eggs, one at a time, beating well after each addition.

In a medium bowl, sift together the flour, baking powder, and salt. Add flour mixture to creamed mixture. Stir until blended.

Place chopped apples in a small bowl. Add ½ of the topping mixture to apples. Stir until apples are coated. Add apples to batter. Pour batter into springform pan. Sprinkle remaining topping over batter.

Bake 1 hour or until cake pulls away from the sides of the pan. Cool on a rack. May be made a day ahead. If kept well wrapped, this cake stays moist for several days.

Fall II

Entrees

Side Dishes

Don't Be Late for School Open House
Or
Pasta and Tuna with Sun-Dried Tomatoes
Serves 6

I don't know why school open houses, band concerts, PTA meetings and other such functions have to begin at 7 p.m. It is almost impossible for the normal family to get home from work, fix a nice dinner, and be at school for a function that begins at 7 p.m. Why don't they start the meetings at 6, so we can go from work to school then have a lovely leisurely dinner at 7:30 or so? Or why not start such events at 8 p.m., so the family can have time to regroup from work, eat a well-balanced meal, *then* attend the meeting?

But the world does not listen to me. So school meetings continue to start at 7 p.m., and I keep trying to find ways to eat a good dinner before racing out of the house.

This dinner is simple to prepare, uses typically on-hand ingredients, and it is delicious served cold the next day for lunch.

½ cup sun-dried tomatoes
½ cup olive oil
2 cloves garlic, minced
¼ teaspoon crushed red pepper
1 pound penne pasta
1 12-ounce can solid white tuna packed in water, drained
⅓ cup sliced black olives
Freshly grated Parmesan cheese

In a small bowl place tomatoes, add enough hot water to cover and soak until soft. Drain. Chop tomatoes. Place in a medium sized bowl with olive oil, garlic, and crushed red pepper.

Cook pasta until done. Drain. Toss with olive oil and tomato mixture. Add tuna and black olives, toss again. Top with Parmesan cheese.

This dish is delicious with bread and a small salad.

"If you love a flower that lives on a star, it is sweet to look at the sky at night."
The Little Prince by Antoine de Saint-Exupery

Easy Fall Dinner

It's Wednesday night and you realize that you're heading towards one of those unusual weekends where you don't have any plans. After a long sigh of relief, you think it might be nice to see your sister and brother-in-law, or your college roommate who you haven't seen since summer, or perhaps some friends who you just haven't had the chance to catch up with since the kids started school. But what to fix for dinner??

Here is a relatively simple fall dinner that can be prepared almost entirely ahead of time.

Marinated Shrimp and Vegetables

Caesar Salad

Butterflied Leg of Lamb
Mashed Potatoes and Parsnip Casserole
Steamed Peas

White and Dark Chocolate Frozen Mousse

Make the mousse several days ahead of time and freeze. Prepare the marinated shrimp at least 2 days in advance and add the vegetables 24 hours before serving.

Marinate the lamb the day before the party.

The morning of the party make the potato and parsnip casserole. Clean the lettuce for the salad.

For a centerpiece purchase one of those funny-looking large squashes that you will find in the produce section of the grocery. Surround the squash with colorful fall leaves you've sent the kids to gather, add a few miniature pumpkins or gourds and you have a beautiful fall table and a beautiful fall dinner.

Butterflied Leg of Lamb
Serves 6

This recipe will serve 6, but I often prefer to serve 4 and ensure plenty of leftovers.

1 leg of lamb (6-6½ pounds), boned and butterflied
⅓ cup olive oil
Juice of 3 lemons
4 large garlic cloves, minced
1 tablespoon chopped, fresh marjoram (1 teaspoon dry)
1 tablespoon chopped, fresh rosemary (1 teaspoon dry)
Salt and pepper
Mint or Jalapeno jelly, optional

Combine oil, lemon juice, garlic, and herbs in a glass baking dish large enough to hold the lamb.

Rub the lamb with salt and pepper, place in dish and turn to coat completely with marinade. Cover and refrigerate for 24 hours, turning the lamb occasionally.

Bring the lamb to room temperature.

Remove lamb from marinade and place it flat on a broiler pan. Broil on low, 6 inches from heat, for 15 minutes. Turn the lamb and broil an additional 15 minutes. Remove from broiler and let stand, covered, for at least 10 minutes.

Slice into ½ inch thick slices. Serve with mint or jalapeno jelly if desired.

This lamb is also delicious when grilled outdoors.

"There is no love sincerer than the love of food."
- **George Bernard Shaw**

Lamb Curry
Serves 4-6

This dish is delicious and a wonderful way to use leftover lamb. Serve on a bed of fluffy rice. Warm applesauce is a good accompaniment. It is one of my children's favorites.

3-4 cups of cooked lamb, cut into 1-inch cubes or bite-sized pieces
2 tablespoons olive oil
2 medium onions, chopped
2 tablespoons flour
2 cups beef broth
½ teaspoon sugar
½ teaspoon salt
1 tablespoon curry powder, or more to taste

In a large saucepan, 3 quarts or more, heat oil. Add chopped onions and sauté until soft. Stir in flour and continue to cook for another minute or more. Whisk in beef broth, stirring constantly. Bring mixture to a boil and stir until liquid begins to thicken. Reduce heat to a simmer. Add sugar, salt, curry, and lamb. Simmer for several minutes to allow flavors to blend.

Serve over rice. May be made the day ahead and also freezes well.

Curry Powder:
A powdered mixture of turmeric, coriander, and other spices. It comes hot or mild. I prefer the mild, but experiment with both to determine which suites your taste best. If the spice bottle is simply marked curry powder, it is usually the mild variety.

Lamb or Beef
Stew*
Serves 4-6

1½-2 pounds cooked lamb, cut into 1 inch pieces (about 2-3
    cups)
2 tablespoons olive oil
1 tablespoon butter
2 medium onions, chopped
3 tablespoons flour
2½ cups beef broth
⅓ cup red wine
1 28-ounce can of tomatoes, chopped with liquid
4 small carrots, peeled and chopped
3-4 small baking potatoes, peeled and chopped
2 cloves garlic, minced
1 tablespoon chopped, fresh thyme leaves, (1 teaspoon dry)
1 tablespoon chopped, fresh rosemary, (1 teaspoon dry)
1 bay leaf
1 teaspoon sugar
1 teaspoon salt
Ground pepper to taste
¾ cup frozen peas

    Cut cooked lamb into 1 inch pieces, removing any
visible fat. Place in bowl and set aside.
    Heat oil and butter over medium heat in a 4-6 quart
stockpot. Add onions and sauté until soft. Add flour and
continue to stir until flour turns a golden brown. Add stock
and wine. Increase heat and continue to stir until mixture
comes to a boil and begins to thicken.
    Reduce heat to a simmer. Add tomatoes, carrots,
potatoes, garlic, thyme, rosemary, bay leaf, sugar, salt, and
pepper. Stir in lamb. Continue to simmer at least 30
minutes, or until potatoes are soft. May be made ahead up
to this point. If time permits, simmer stew 1-2 hours to
develop flavors.
    About 15 minutes before serving, stir in frozen peas.

Leftovers are excellent frozen and put away for another busy night.

* To make Beef Stew, substitute cooked beef, such as sirloin or roast, for cooked lamb and leave out the rosemary.

Potato and Parsnip Casserole
Serves 6

2 pounds potatoes
½ pound parsnips
1 cup lowfat cottage cheese
1 cup sour cream
3 tablespoons finely diced onion
2 tablespoons butter, melted
1 teaspoon salt
Ground pepper to taste
3 egg whites, beaten until stiff

Preheat oven to 350 degrees. Grease 2-quart casserole dish. Peel and roughly chop potatoes and parsnips. Bring a large pot of salted water to a boil. Add potatoes and parsnips. Boil until soft. Drain and mash.

Place mashed potatoes and parsnips in a medium bowl. Add cottage cheese, sour cream, diced onion, melted butter, salt, and pepper. Stir until well blended. Fold in beaten egg whites. Pour into casserole dish and bake about 1 hour or until top begins to brown.

Casserole may be assembled several hours ahead of time and kept refrigerated until ready to bake.

Christopher Columbus Day Dinner

Antipasti – consisting of grapes, an assortment of Italian cheese (such as fontina and gorgonzola), fresh figs if available, and few slice of prosciutto – Serve with Italian bread.

Paella

Apple Pie

Christopher Columbus Day is a wonderful holiday to celebrate with food.   It is a great opportunity to teach the kids a little bit about Italian, Spanish and American cuisine.   Christopher Columbus was born in Italy, he sailed under the Spanish flag and discovered America.   So in celebrating his day, why not celebrate with food from the countries he represents.

This Christopher Columbus Dinner party is more fun than the best sale at any department store.   Let the children invite a friend or two for dinner.   It will be an evening of fun and entertainment for all ages.

To set the mood for dinner, have the children make explorer hats out of newspaper or brown paper bags for each dinner guest.   Make place cards with the Italian, Spanish or the American flag on it – along with the guest's name.   Use a globe for the centerpiece, and everyone is ready to sail the seven seas.

Pass the antipasti on a tray and let each guest take a sample of whatever they like.   Children love all the options on an antipasti tray and will usually eat more than one would estimate.   As the first course is passed, ask each guest to tell something about the country, represented by the flag on their place card – and what role did that country play in the discovery of America.   Conversation is usually fascinating with the children's understanding of the discovery of America.

170

When the evening is over, everyone will probably know a little more about food, Christopher Columbus, and what makes life good.

To Assemble Dinner

Make the apple pie in the morning or up to two weeks in advance and freeze. The antipasti tray may be assembled several hours in advance and kept refrigerated. If made immediately before the party, the paella will keep up to an hour in a warm oven.

Paella
Serves 6

Paella is probably the most famous Spanish dish in America. This version is a wonderful mixture of seafood, chicken and pork. There is something for everyone in it and it is quite simple to make.

A paella pan is not necessary, all that is required is a skillet 12 inches or larger. For best results – have all ingredients chopped, measured and ready-to-go before beginning the cooking process.

¼ cup olive oil
1 pound boneless, skinless chicken, about 3 breasts
1 large onion chopped
1 red bell pepper, chopped
3 garlic cloves, crushed
2 cups long-grain rice
3 cups chicken stock
1 cup dry white wine
2 ripe tomatoes, peeled and diced
Pinch of saffron
1 tablespoon sweet paprika
¼ teaspoon crushed red pepper
½ pound cooked ham cut in ½ inch cubes – or ½ pound
    Kielbasa sausage cut in ¼ inch slices
1 cup frozen peas
⅓ pound red snapper or cod, cut into bite-size pieces
½ pound shrimp, peeled and cleaned
10 – 12 small clams or mussels, in their shells

In a large, 12-inch skillet heat the oil. Brown the chicken, remove to a platter and cut chicken into bite-size pieces. Set aside. Add the onions and peppers to the skillet and cook over medium heat until soft, do not brown. Add the garlic and rice, cook, stirring until the grains are transparent and the oil is absorbed. Add stock, wine, tomatoes, saffron, paprika, crushed pepper, ham, chicken, peas and salt and pepper to taste.

Bring the liquid to a boil, reduce to a simmer. Cover and continue to cook over a low heat for 15 minutes, stirring occasionally. Add fish. Cover and continue to cook for an additional 10 minutes or until most of the liquid has been absorbed and the rice is tender. If the liquid is absorbed before the rice is tender, add more water or chicken stock.

Set shrimp and clams on top of paella. Cover and continue to cook for 10 minutes.*

Pass the skillet and let guests choose their own dinner from the paella.

*The clam or mussel shells should have opened after ten minutes. However, sometimes they don't. If the shells have not opened after ten minutes, removed paella from heat. Take clams out, and place them in a pot with about 1 inch of boiling water. Cover and steam clams (or mussels) for 3- 5 minutes. Place opened clams on top of paella and serve. Discard any shells that do not open after this process.

For Variation – alter the amount of meat, fish or shellfish to suit your taste. Total weight of meat and fish should be about 3 pounds.

A Fancy Fall Dinner for Four

There are a lot of birthdays and anniversaries in our family during the cool months. This menu is nice in that it can be made smaller for a romantic dinner of two or enlarged for a gathering of six or more.

Grapes, cheese, and assorted olives

Butternut Squash Soup with Sorrel and Curry Puree

**Breast of Duck with Blueberry Sauce on Polenta
Green Bean Bundles**

Pears Poached in Wine with Whipped Cream

Bunches of grapes on a silver tray make a lovely fall presentation. Add an assortment of cheeses, crackers and a variety of olives to complete the appetizer selection.

The pears and the polenta may be made the day ahead and kept refrigerated. The soup and the green bean bundles may be made the morning of the party. The blueberry sauce may also be made ahead if desired.

The only last minute preparation should be to sauté and bake the duck breasts and finish cooking the beans.

Breast of Duck with Blueberry Sauce on Polenta

Serves 4

Duck is a wonderful food, and a delicious alternative to chicken and beef. It is easy to prepare and a great dish for entertaining. Breast of duck is often packaged separately in the frozen food section of the grocery. If not, ask your butcher where or how to locate it.

2 breasts of duck (about ¾ pound each)
2 tablespoons olive oil

Blueberry Sauce
2 cups frozen or fresh blueberries
½ cup sugar
½ cup chicken stock
¼ cup port wine
¼ teaspoon grated lemon zest

Polenta – see recipe

Make polenta several hours ahead or the day before.
Preheat oven to 275 degrees. Place four slices of polenta (about 1 inch thick) on an oven-proof plate.
In a large skillet, heat oil over medium-high heat. Salt and pepper duck breasts. Place duck breast (one-at-a-time if both do not fit) in skillet and brown on both sides. Remove breasts to oven–proof plate and place in oven to finish cooking for 30 minutes. Also place polenta slices in oven at this time.
While the duck and polenta are in oven, make blueberry sauce. In a small sauce pan place blueberries, sugar, stock, port and lemon zest. Bring to a boil, then reduce heat to a simmer. Continue to simmer, stirring occasionally, for 20 – 30 minutes. Sauce should have reduced and thickened slightly.

Remove duck breasts from oven and carve in slices. Take drippings from plate holding the duck breasts and pour into the blueberry sauce. Bring sauce back to a boil for 1 – 2 minutes.

Assemble plates. Puddle a tablespoon or 2 of sauce on each plate. Top sauce with a slice of warm polenta. Arrange slices of duck breast on top of polenta.

Polenta
Serves 8 – 10

There is something wonderful about the experience of making polenta. I don't know why standing over a pot of boiling meal for 30 or so minutes is enjoyable, but it is when making polenta. There is just something about those little grains of cornmeal turning into a creamy, delicious mass. You can buy instant polenta, and you may purchase polenta already made – but for a satisfying experience, both physical and sensual – make your own polenta.

Polenta is a great dish. It may be eaten warm with a little butter as a side dish. Or, it may be made ahead, then sliced for numerous uses. The slices may be broiled with cheese on top (try Fontina, Swiss or Parmesan). Then serve these delicious cheese sticks with grilled meats or fish.

The slices may also be used as a bed for a meat and sauce (our favorite). Heat the slices in an oven. Puddle a sauce (such as blueberry) on the plate, top with a slice of warm polenta, then add slices of meat (such as duck or chicken).

Lastly, the slices may be fried in butter and served with bacon and eggs for breakfast.

I grew up in the Midwest eating mush for breakfast. No one ever called it polenta. It was many years later that I learned the two were the same, and I could make it myself. I never will forget impressing my father one year when I made polenta for dinner (something he had never heard of) and mush for breakfast!

This recipe is adapted from Marcella Hazan's Essentials of Classic Italian Cooking.

7 cups water
1 teaspoon salt
1 2/3 cups yellow cornmeal

In a large heavy pot, at least 4 quarts, bring the water and salt to a boil. Over a medium high heat, begin to add the cornmeal in a slow, thin stream. Continue to whisk the mixture as you add the cornmeal. When all the cornmeal has been added, use a long-handle wooden spoon and continue to stir and cook the cornmeal mixture. Continue to cook and stir for 30 to 40 minutes or until the cornmeal becomes polenta and forms a mass that pulls cleanly away from the sides of the pot.

If serving immediately, spoon onto plates. If making ahead, place polenta in an 8x8 inch baking dish. After cooling for several hours, the polenta may be sliced directly out of the baking dish, or the dish may be inverted onto a wooden board and sliced from there.

Polenta will keep for several days in the refrigerator, wrapped in plastic wrap.

To clean the pot used to make polenta: After removing polenta, fill pot with water. Let the pot soak overnight. The next day most of the cornmeal film in pot will lift out easily.

Green Bean Bundles

These little vegetables bundles are as pretty to look at as they are delicious to eat. They are especially attractive for entertaining in that they may be assembled ahead of time. I prefer fresh green beans, but frozen may be substituted. For Christmas, trying sticking a slice of red bell pepper in the bundle. Recipe is from friend Debbie Vaky.

Allow a small handful of green beans per person
Green tops of scallions

Clean beans, leave whole. Rinse scallion tops. In a large pot, bring water to boil. While water is heating, place cold water and ice cubes in a medium mixing bowl.

Put green beans in boiling water and blanch for 2 minutes. Remove with a slotted spoon and place immediately in ice water to stop the cooking process.

In the same boiling water, place scallion tops. Blanch for 1 – 2 minutes. Remove to a paper towel to drain. When green beans have cooled, also place on a paper towel to drain.

Arrange green beans in bundles (1 serving each bundle). Tie each bundle with a scallion top. The thinner the scallion top, the easier it is to tie.

Place the bundles in a single layer in a greased baking dish. Beans may be made ahead and kept refrigerated for several hours at this point.

Preheat oven to 275 degrees. Drizzle beans with melted butter or olive oil. Sprinkle with salt and pepper. Bake 30 minutes.

These bundles are so pretty, I like to serve them on a separate bread and butter plate with a small slice of lemon.

Meatloaf
Serves 6

Meatloaf is truly a meal that I believe one should "create". Although there are recipes for making meatloaf, I think it is best if each individual develop their own style and technique for cooking this American favorite.

Once created, the loaf may be baked in a baking dish or a loaf pan. I prefer a baking pan in that the fat renders itself to the bottom of the pan – making a leaner version than the one baked in a loaf pan.

The toppings for meatloaf are also a creation. I like swirls of ketchup with garnishes of green bell pepper slices. Olives, mustard or whatever sounds good to you may also be used to decorate the top before baking.

The following guidelines may be used for 3 pounds of meat. A 3 pound meatloaf should provide about 6 servings.

3 pounds of ground meat – a combination of beef, pork and veal is the most traditional. Ground chicken or turkey may also be used in the combination.

1 medium onion, chopped
1 slice bread, broken into pieces and soaked in ⅓ cup
    milk
1 egg beaten

After this point everything else is up to the chef.
Listed below are some of our favorite meatloaf ingredients:
Ketchup – about ¼ cup
Worcestershire Sauce, a dash or two
Tabasco, a drop or two
Minced garlic, a large pinch
Chopped green bell pepper, if I have some on hand
Chopped celery, if I am in the mood
Salt, about a teaspoon
Lots of fresh ground pepper

Gently combine all meatloaf ingredients. Form a loaf. Decorate top, if desired. Bake at 350 degree for about an hour or until loaf registers 160 degrees. Let stand at least 10 minutes before slicing.

Our favorite accompaniments to meatloaf are mashed potatoes and peas. Meatloaf sandwiches are also delicious the next day for lunch.

Use your hands to mix the meatloaf!!! Clean hands are probably the best mixing utensil you have. This is also a wonderful way for the kids to have fun and help prepare dinner.

Thanksgiving Dinner

I really don't quite remember how many Thanksgivings I've spent cooking from sunrise to sunset – only to finally sit down, give thanks, and have the children announce they were not eating anything!! It all tasted yucky!

How could that be? It was my mother's candied sweet potatoes, the ones I loved. It was her wonderful stuffing with giblet gravy. How could my children not love this?

Then I finally realized this is not the type of food we normally eat. I guess the only time I ever made stuffing was at Thanksgiving. It is a food the children are not accustomed to eating, especially laden with giblets and butter.

"The pilgrims would never eat this stuff," my third grader announced one year.

What did the pilgrims eat? The following November I took all three of the little darlings to the library in an effort to determine what our Forefathers really did eat at the first Thanksgiving.

We learned that the early settlers fished and hunted. So we thought they probably would have eaten some type of fish. And the turkey, if it was stuffed with anything, was probably filled with some fresh herbs.
We know the bird was cooked on a spit over a large fire, not in an oven.

After several hours of research, this is the menu we developed to represent a "True Thanksgiving Dinner", and one that we all ate.

Ask your children to help create your Thanksgiving dinner. It is amazing how much better food tastes when you have had a hand in the planning.

Thanksgiving Dinner Menu

Tray of smoked fish, cheese, fruit, crackers

New England Clam Chowder

Grilled Turkey
Sweet Potato and Apple Tart
Steamed Brussel Sprouts and Onions
Della's Cranberry Compote
Cornbread

Pumpkin Pie
Pecan Pie

Grilled Turkey

An 8 – 10 pound turkey will serve 8 guests with plenty of leftovers. To estimate cooking, allow about 15 minutes per pound. I recommend using a meat thermometer to determine when the bird is done. For turkey, it should register 175 – 180 degrees.

"Certainly there are few things worse than an overcooked turkey, except perhaps an undercooked one."
- **James Beard**

Cook the turkey using indirect heat. Bank the coals on the side of the grill and put a drip pan in the center of the grill under the bird. Keep the grill covered while cooking.

After preparing the grill, rinse and pat dry the turkey. Make sure it is at room temperature before cooking. Rub inside and out with salt and pepper. Stuff the bird with any available herbs, such as parsley, thyme and oregano.

Baste the bird with the following sauce during cooking. Let the turkey rest at least 15 – 20 minutes before carving. The turkey may be served warm or at room temperature.

Basting Sauce for Grilled Turkey

½ cup olive oil
¼ cup dry white wine
 1 – 2 bay leaves
Juice of ½ lemon
1 tablespoon butter, melted
1 teaspoon garlic powder
¼ teaspoon onion powder
½ teaspoon Italian Seasoning
¼ teaspoon dry basil leaves
2 teaspoons fresh oregano leaves, roughly chopped
1 teaspoon fresh thyme leaves

1 teaspoon fresh rosemary leaves
Freshly ground pepper and salt to taste

In a medium bowl place olive oil, wine, bay leaves, lemon juice, melted butter, garlic powder, onion powder, Italian seasoning and basil. Stir to combine. Add fresh herbs of oregano, thyme and rosemary.

Generously baste turkey with sauce every 20 minutes or so during the cooking process.

Before there were thermometers, women tested the heat of their oven by seeing how long they could hold their hand in them.

Brussel Sprouts and Onions
Serves 8

Brussel Sprouts are my favorite fall vegetable. Their best flavor comes after the first frost. Choose brussels that are less than an inch in diameter. Choose ones that feel firm and heavy. Avoid any that have wilting or yellowing leaves, or do not hold a tight head.

Fresh brussel sprouts are delicious plain, simply steamed. They are made even better with a drizzle of olive oil or butter. Small pearl onions are my favorite companion for them.

Brussels may also be dressed-up with chestnuts or toasted chopped walnuts.

2 pounds brussel sprouts
1 pound pearl onions, peeled

To clean brussels, rise, cut off stems and cut an X in the bottom of each.

Steam onions and brussels together until tender, approximately 10 minutes. Drizzle with olive oil or melted butter. Season with salt and pepper. Toss lightly until coated. Serve warm.

Sweet Potato and Apple Tart
Serves 8

2 pounds sweet potatoes or yams
2 tablespoons butter
⅓ cup brown sugar
2 tablespoons cream sherry
1 teaspoon cinnamon
¼ teaspoon salt
2 apples, such as Granny Smith, peeled and sliced
2 tablespoons orange marmalade

Bake sweet potatoes in a 350 degree oven for 1 hour or until tender. Peel potatoes. Place in a food processor or blender. Add butter, brown sugar, sherry, cinnamon and salt. Puree until smooth.

Grease a quiche pan. Smooth potatoes into quiche pan. Peel and slice apples. Working in a circle, place apples in a single layer on top of potatoes. Recipe may be made ahead up to this point. Keep refrigerated until ready to bake.

Preheat oven to 350 degrees. Bake casserole approximately 30 minutes. Remove from oven. Melt marmalade in the microwave. Brush on top of apples. Serve.

This dish is attractive as well as delicious and is well suited for buffets. It is excellent served with pork, turkey or chicken.

Sweet potatoes are one of the most complete foods available to the consumer. Rich in vitamins, this native American vegetable is one food of which we all should be eating more.

Della's Cranberry Compote
Serves 8

This is my mother-in-law's recipe. It is a required dish at all their Thanksgivings, and I like it because it is made in advance and has a nice fresh taste.

3 apples, with skin, cored and cut into chunks
3 oranges, with skin, cut into chunks, seeds removed
1 pound cranberries, rinsed and picked over
2 cups sugar.

Place apples, oranges, and cranberries in a food processor; may be done in batches. Process until evenly chopped. Or: run cranberries, oranges, and apples through a meat grinder.

Pour processed fruit into a glass container and stir in sugar. Refrigerate at least 48 hours before serving.

Compote: n. 1. fruit stewed in a syrup. 2. a dish having a stem, used for serving fruit, nuts, etc.
- The Random House Dictionary

Sausage, Peppers and Pasta
Serves 6-8

This is a great recipe for family and guests. All that is needed to complete the meal is a fresh salad, crusty bread, and a bottle of red wine.

1 pound sweet Italian sausage links
3 tablespoons olive oil
1 medium onion, chopped
3 red bell peppers, stems, ribs, and seeds removed, cut into
   ½ inch chunks
5 garlic cloves, peeled and finely chopped
1 28-ounce can of tomatoes, chopped with liquid
1 15-ounce can of tomatoes, chopped with liquid
1 tablespoon dried oregano leaves
1 teaspoon dried thyme leaves
1 teaspoon crushed red pepper
1 teaspoon fennel seeds
1 teaspoon salt
Freshly ground pepper to taste
¼ cup chopped, fresh Italian parsley
1 pound pasta (we like penne with this dish)

Prick sausage links all over with a fork and put them in a pot or large skillet with ½ inch of water. Set the pot over medium heat and simmer the sausages, uncovered, in the water for about 20 minutes. Eventually the pot will boil dry and the sausages will begin to fry in their own fat. Turn them occasionally and cook for another 10 minutes or until they are brown.

Remove sausages from the pot and drain on a paper towel. Pour sausage fat out of pan but do not wash it. Set pan over low heat, add olive oil then onions. Simmer until onions are soft. Add bell peppers, and cook for 5 more minutes, stirring often. Add garlic. Add wine, tomatoes, oregano, thyme, fennel, red pepper, and salt and pepper to taste.

Simmer, partially covered for about 30 minutes. While sauce is simmering, cook the pasta.

Slice the sausages into ¼ inch round slices. Add sliced sausage to the tomato mixture. Add parsley and simmer 10 more minutes. Serve over pasta.

Pass freshly grated Parmesan cheese to sprinkle on top if desired.

What is a Serving???

Is it the amount my 12-year-old eats of Sausage, Peppers and Pasta? Or is it the amount I serve the guest? Or could it possibly be the amount my 8-year-old daughter eats? I don't have the answer.

A cooking instructor once told me a serving was ½ a cup. I have not been able to document this, but even if it is true, is it a ½ cup for meats, pastas, and vegetables??? I can eat ½ cup of pasta, but I'm not so certain about ½ cup of okra!

Consequently, a lot of the recipes in this cookbook have a range for the number of servings in the dish.

Chunky Style Applesauce
Serves 4-6

I received this recipe from my son's second grade teacher, and although the teacher was not much to rave about, this recipe certainly is.

There is something wonderful about the smell of cinnamon and apples cooking. By using a crockpot, the magic smell begins in the morning and invades the house all day. By nightfall we are all starved for a fall dinner highlighted by homemade applesauce.

This is probably the only recipe for which I use my crockpot, but it is so good that it is worth purchasing a crockpot just to make this applesauce.

8-10 cooking apples, peeled, cored, and cut into chunks
½ cup water
1 teaspoon cinnamon
1/2 – 1 cup sugar (depending on the sweetness of the apples)

Put all ingredients into a crockpot and cook on low for 6-8 hours. Serve warm. If you are in a hurry, the applesauce may be made in 1-2 hours by placing the crockpot on high setting.

Make Your Own Pizza
Serves 4

There is something very special about making your own pizza. Maybe it's the crust, or perhaps the fresh ingredients make it so delicious. Or maybe, it's because you're the one deciding just how much cheese or tomato sauce tastes good. Whatever the reason, making your own pizza is definitely worth the experience.

My children love to make their own pizza and they always ask if they can bring a friend over for dinner as soon as I start making the dough. Thus, I usually double this recipe to ensure there is plenty of dough for unexpected guests. Plus, we all like leftover, cold pizza for breakfast or lunch the next day.

This is Wolfgang Puck's recipe. The recipe makes 4 8-inch pizzas so each person can create their own pizza masterpiece.

Making the dough takes a little forethought and preparation, but the results are well worth the time and effort.

Be sure to provide a wide variety of toppings, and make sure there is plenty to go around!

Pizza Dough:

1 package fresh or dry yeast
¼ cup warm water
Pinch of sugar
1 teaspoon salt
1 tablespoon honey
2 tablespoons olive oil
¾ cup cool water
3 cups all-purpose flour

Dissolve yeast in ¼ cup warm water with a pinch of sugar and let proof for 10 minutes.

In a small bowl, combine salt, honey, olive oil, and cool water. Stir to blend.

In a large mixing bowl place flour and make a well in the center. Pour honey-water mixture and proofed yeast into the well. Slowly incorporate flour into wet ingredients. When dough is formed, transfer to a lightly floured surface and knead until smooth (Or, I use my mixer with a dough hook and beat for 35 seconds). Place ball of dough in a greased bowl, let rest, covered, for 30 minutes.

Divide dough into four equal parts. Roll into smooth, tight balls. Place on a flat dish or baking sheet, cover with a damp towel. Refrigerate at least 2 hours. Dough may be made up to a day in advance at this point.

One hour before baking, remove dough from refrigerator and let sit, covered, at room temperature.

Lightly flour work surface. Roll out each ball of dough into a circle about 6 inches in diameter, making the outer edges a little thicker than the center. Lift the dough and gently stretch the edges, working clockwise to form an 8-inch circle. (Make the crust thicker or thinner depending on your personal taste.)

Before you are ready to bake the pizzas, preheat a pizza stone in a 500 degree oven for 30 minutes. Brush each pizza crust with olive oil to prevent other ingredients from leaking through to the crust. Top individual pizzas with desired ingredients. Bake pizzas at 500 degrees on the pizza stone for 10-12 minutes.

If you don't have a pizza stone, the pizzas may also be baked on a pizza pan in the oven.

Our Favorite Pizza Toppings:
Mozzarella, goat cheese, Parmesan cheese, sliced fresh tomatoes, bell peppers, jalapeno peppers, mushrooms, sliced eggplant, onions, pepperoni, cooked sausage, crisp bacon, anchovies, green and black olives, fresh herbs, Italian seasoning, and of course tomato sauce.

Fall III

Desserts

Pumpkin Cookies
Makes about 3 dozen cookies

Maybe they don't sound too tasty, but these cookies are wonderful. My daughter's birthday falls near Halloween and she insisted on taking these cookies every year of elementary school to celebrate her special day. They have been such a hit that numerous teachers have asked for the recipe.

Pumpkin cookies are the perfect dessert for a Halloween party, or any fall party for that matter.

Cookies:
1 cup sugar
8 tablespoons butter, softened (1 stick)
1 cup canned pumpkin
1 tablespoon grated fresh orange peel, or 1½ teaspoon dried
2 cups flour
1 teaspoon baking powder
1 teaspoon baking soda
1 teaspoon cinnamon
¼ teaspoon salt
1 cup raisins, or 1 cup chocolate chips, or ½ cup of each

Glaze:
4 tablespoons butter
2 cups powdered sugar
1 teaspoon vanilla
Several tablespoons milk

To Make Cookies:
Preheat oven to 375 degrees. Cream sugar and butter together until smooth. Add pumpkin and orange peel, mix.

In a medium bowl sift together flour, baking powder, baking soda, cinnamon and salt. Stir pumpkin mixture into flour mixture. Stir in raisins and/or chocolate chips.

Drop cookie dough, by teaspoons, onto an ungreased cookie sheet. Bake until bottoms begin to brown, about 8-10 minutes. When cookies have cooled, spread with glaze.

To Make Glaze:

Melt butter in a small skillet and continue to cook until butter turn a golden brown. Do not burn. Remove from heat.

Place browned butter in a bowl with powdered sugar. Stir in vanilla. With a whisk, stir in milk, one tablespoon at a time, until glaze becomes a spreadable mixture. Spread glaze over top of cookies.

Challenge your taste buds. Make the eaters guess what the cookies are made of- make them guess what is inside the cookie: is it a chocolate chip or a raisin or both? The more we think about what we eat, the better educated eaters and tasters we will be.

<u>Our favorite Halloween Parties Have</u>:

Little plastic bugs frozen in the ice cubes

Feely boxes with cold spaghetti that feels like intestines

Feely boxes with peeled grapes that we think are eyeballs

Teachers and Moms and Dads who don't wear scary costumes

Pears Poached in Wine
Serves 6

Poached pears are as impressive to look at as they are delicious to eat. Choose pears that are slightly under-ripe and ones with a long stem for poaching. Bartlett and Bosc varieties work well.

I prefer to serve the pears chilled as a side dish to a roast chicken or pork. They are equally delicious, however, served as a dessert topped with a dollop of whipped cream or chocolate sauce.

6 pears
2½ cups red wine
1½ cups sugar
2 whole peppercorns
2 cloves
1 stick vanilla bean, or 1 teaspoon vanilla extract
Juice of 1 lemon

In a large saucepan that can hold the six pears, place the wine, sugar, spices, and lemon juice. Bring to a boil. Peel the pears, leaving the stem intact, and place in the boiling syrup. Reduce heat to a simmer and cook the pears for 10 minutes or until tender when pierced with a fork. Baste the pears with the juice and turn occasionally while cooking.

Remove pears to a platter on which they will be served. Reduce remaining liquid by half. Spoon several tablespoons of the reduced juice over the pears. I prefer to bring the platter of pears to the table to serve.

Serve warm or refrigerate until cool. Pears may be prepared a day ahead and kept refrigerated.

If serving as a dessert, try whipped cream, chocolate sauce, or ice cream as a garnish.

Apple Pie
Serves 6

Is there anything better than a homemade apple pie on a crisp autumn day?

6-8 baking apples such as granny smith or pippin, peeled, cored, and sliced (about 4 heaping cups of sliced apples)
½ cup white sugar
¼ cup brown sugar
2 tablespoons flour
1 teaspoon cinnamon
Dash of freshly ground nutmeg
Dash of salt
2 tablespoons butter, cut into ¼ inch slices
Pastry for two 9-inch pie crusts (p.145)

Preheat oven to 425 degrees. In a large bowl toss apples with sugars. Stir in flour, cinnamon, nutmeg, and salt. Line a 9-inch pie pan with dough. Pour apples mixture into pan, top with sliced butter. Cover with remaining pie dough. Seal and flute the edges. With a sharp knife, place slits in the center of dough to allow steam to escape.
Bake 40 minutes or until golden brown and the center is bubbling.

Mom and Apple Pie:
They represent America; the best we are in the most simple form. May we pay tribute to them often.

Pumpkin Pie
Serves 6

This is my mother's pumpkin pie recipe. She swears the secret is in the browned butter. I'm not sure if that's the case, but it is a very good pumpkin pie.

Pastry for one 9-inch pie crust (p.145)
2 eggs
1 cup milk
1 tablespoon butter
1 cup canned pumpkin
⅓ cup granulated sugar
2½ teaspoons cinnamon
½ teaspoon salt
¼ teaspoon ginger
¼ teaspoon ground nutmeg

Preheat oven to 450 degrees. Line a pie plate with pastry crust. Flute the edges. Set in the refrigerator until ready to fill.

In a medium bowl, beat eggs and milk together. In a small skillet, melt butter over medium heat and continue to cook and swirl until butter turns a golden brown. Add browned butter to milk and egg mixture.

Add pumpkin, sugars, cinnamon, salt, ginger, and nutmeg to egg and milk mixture. Stir to combine.

Pour mixture into pie shell. Bake at 450 degrees for 10 minutes then reduce heat to 300 degrees and bake an additional 45 minutes or until set.

"On the bank of the stream they found Ichabod's hat. Close beside it was a shattered pumpkin. They searched the brook, but did not find the schoolmaster's body."
- The Legend of Sleepy Hollow by Washington Irving

Pecan Pie
Serves 6

Native to the United States, pecans have become a traditional repast of American Thanksgiving Dinners. Additionally, they are delicious in pies, ice cream, pralines, and various stuffings for turkey and goose.

Pastry for one 9-inch pie crust (p.145)
3 eggs
½ cup white sugar
½ cup brown sugar
1 cup light corn syrup
1 cup shelled pecans
3 tablespoons melted butter
1 tablespoon vanilla extract

Preheat oven to 450 degrees. Line pie pan with pastry crust and flute the edges. Set in refrigerator until ready to fill.

In a medium mixing bowl beat eggs. Add sugars and corn syrup. Stir to combine. Add pecans, melted butter, and vanilla. Stir. Pour mixture into pie shell.

Bake for 10 minutes then reduce heat to 325 degrees and continue baking for an additional 35 minutes or until pie is set. Cool on rack.

Serve plain or with a scoop of ice cream or whipped cream.

"It's Your Wish"
Dinner Party

This is one of my children's favorite dinners. Usually held the first Sunday after Thanksgiving, everyone in the family is invited to dinner and requested to bring their Christmas "wish list".

We started this annual dinner sometime after the kids decided they were too old to write letters to Santa.

Even my husband, who refused to bring a list the first couple of years, has gotten into the fun of sharing Christmas dreams at the dinner table. Each year our lists seem to get a little more exotic and much more humorous.

It's an evening filled with jokes and laughter, wants, desires, dreams, and – of course – good food.

Caesar Salad Sans Egg

Sausage Peppers and Pasta
Italian Bread

Chocolate Dream Pie

Chocolate Dream Pie
Serves 8

This rich chocolate pie with a cookie-like crust is one of my favorites. This recipe is from Gail McClean, a neighbor and friend when my husband I were first married and living in Baltimore.

Crust:
½ cup brown sugar
1 cup flour
½ cup chopped pecans
4 tablespoons butter (½ stick), softened

Filling:
½ pound butter (2 sticks) softened
1 ½ cup sugar
2 teaspoons vanilla
½ teaspoon almond extract
3 ounces unsweetened chocolate, melted
4 eggs
Pinch of salt

To Make the Crust:
Preheat the oven to 400 degrees. In a small bowl mix together the sugar, flour, nuts, and butter. Pat mixture down in a 9x13 inch pan. Bake 15 minutes. Break up the crust. Pour broken crust into a 9-inch pie pan and pat into bottom and sides. Refrigerate.

To Make the Filling:
Cream together the butter and sugar until light and fluffy. Beat in vanilla, almond extract, and melted chocolate. Add eggs, one at a time, beating well after each addition. Add a pinch of salt. Spoon filling into crust. Refrigerate several hours before serving.

To Melt Chocolate:

I have found that the easiest and most successful way to melt a small amount of chocolate is to put the chocolate in a bowl and microwave it for about 1 minute, or until melted. The more traditional way of melting chocolate is to place the chocolate in the top of a double broiler and stir until melted.

White and Dark Chocolate Frozen Mousse

Serves 6

1 envelope unflavored gelatin (2 tablespoons)
¾ cup sugar
¾ cup water
4 egg yolks, slightly beaten
4 egg whites
1 cup whipping cream
6 ounces semi-sweet chocolate, melted
6 ounces white chocolate, melted
½ teaspoon vanilla
¼ teaspoon lemon juice
Fresh berries (optional), as garnish

In a medium saucepan, combine gelatin and sugar. Stir in water and egg yolks. Cook and stir over medium heat until gelatin dissolves. Bring gently to a boil (be careful or egg yolks will scramble), continue to cook and stir for an additional 2 minutes. Remove from heat and cover with plastic wrap or wax paper. (This prevents a skin from forming on the top.) Cool to room temperature.

Beat egg whites until stiff. Fold egg whites into cooled gelatin mixture. Beat cream until it forms stiff peaks. Fold cream into gelatin mixture. Divide mixture into two equal portions.

Melt semi-sweet chocolate either in the microwave or on top of a double broiler. Fold melted semi-sweet chocolate into one portion of the gelatin mixture. Pour this semi-sweet chocolate mixture into the bottom of an 8x4 inch loaf pan. Refrigerate until partially set, about 30 minutes.

Melt the white chocolate. Fold into the remaining gelatin mixture. Stir in vanilla and lemon juice. When semi-sweet mixture has partially set, pour the white chocolate mixture over it. Cool and freeze until firm.

Unmold and cut into 1 inch wide slices. Garnish with fresh berries if desired.

May be made ahead and frozen up to a week or so.

Instead of putting the mousse in the freezer, it may be placed in the refrigerator and chilled until set. A refrigerated mousse has a creamier texture. Try both ways.

Winter

Winter dances into our lives with parties, gifts, and a spectacular array of food.

We eat better and more elaborately than we've eaten all year. Even people who never cook seem to turn out beautiful buffets and platefuls of homemade cookies.

It is a wonderful time of year, and a wonderful time to celebrate food. We eat, we drink, and we are merry.

But winter is also a time of cold, of grey skies, and lonely days. We need lots of comfort, and lots of comfort food: plenty of chili and homemade soups and breads.

It is a great time of year to cook and to entertain, and a time to sit by the fire with family and friends.

Winter I

Appetizers

Soups

Salads

Breads

Breakfast Foods

Holiday Dinner Party for 16

Cold Glazed Salmon with Sweet Mustard Dill Sauce
Vegetable Christmas Tree
Sun-Dried Tomato Canapés

Crab Cakes with Roasted Red Bell Pepper Sauce

Beef Tenderloin
Winter Vegetables with Horseradish Sauce
Coucous

Chocolate Mousse Dacquoise

This is a very special dinner party. Yes, it is a lot of work – but the party is one of the most spectacular and fun dinners I have given. Most importantly, the majority of the food may be prepared ahead of time so the host or hostess may serve the dinner with style, grace and relaxation.

Sixteen people is a lot of people for one person to serve – so I employ the help of the gentlemen at the party. The arrangement really makes for a fun evening and is one worth trying. It has the additional benefit of forcing guests to mingle and is a huge help to the hostess.

Divide the guests among three tables. I usually set one table in the dinning room, one in the family room and one in the living room. For the holiday, I use white tablecloths, napkins and candles. For flowers, I fill brandy glasses with holly and white carnations. Group the glasses in the center or spread them up and down the table.

Serve cocktails and appetizers in whichever room there is enough space.

Make sure there are placards on the tables for each guest. I usually start the meal with each husband and wife sitting next to each other.

As the guests sit down to eat the first course of crab cakes, explain to them that the men will be required to clear the plates at their table.

When everyone is done eating the first course, the men clear the plates. Then each gentleman must find a seat at another table. Each sir takes with him only his napkin and wine glass. The women remain seated throughout the meal. (The hostess, however, does have to get up to prepare the plates for the next course.)

Each man must move to the different table, it doesn't matter which table, as long as it is not the same one where he ate the first course. Once they have found a new seat, the men then serve that table the main course. When everyone is finished with the main course, the gentlemen again clear the plates – then move to a third table and serve dessert.

Additional silverware should not be necessary as long as the guest use the salad fork for the first course, the place knife and fork for the main course, and a dessert fork for dessert.

Everyone is usually into the spirit of clearing and serving by the third course, and entertainment, conversation and comedy abound.

My husband and I first learned of this procedure at a rehearsal dinner party. The groom, who was from Scotland, said the males switching tables after each course was a custom at weddings there. My husband and I thought it would be a great idea to put the gentlemen to work clearing and serving while they were busy switching tables and meeting guests.

Conversely, the women could do the serving and the men stay seated. It's up to the host or hostess.

The Game Plan

Cold Glazed Salmon – Prepare the day before the party. Finish the morning of the party. Prepare the sauce 2 – 3 days in advance.

Vegetable Christmas Tree – Prepare the day before the party. If making your own dressing, also make several days in advance.

Sun-Dried Tomato Canapés – Make several weeks in advance and freeze.

Crab Cakes – Prepare and broil the morning of the party. Reheat in 350 degree oven for approximately 15 minutes or until warm. Make the base of the sauce the day before, finish with additional butter just before serving.

Winter Vegetables – Steam vegetables in the morning of the party and reheat in 350 degree oven for 10 – 15 minutes. Make the sauce five days in advance and refrigerate. Reheat and pour hot sauce on vegetables right before serving.

Coucous – Prepare during cocktails. It will remain warm until time to serve.

Beef Tenderloin – Beef may be made ahead of time, covered, and left standing for up to an hour.

Chocolate Mousse Dacquoise – Make meringues 5 days in advance. Wrap in plastic wrap and store in an air-tight container. Make mousse and whip cream one day in advance and assemble the dessert the morning of the party.

Cold Glazed Salmon
Serves 8 – 10

This is without a doubt the most spectacular appetizer I know. Not only is it beautiful to look at, but delicious as well. It has become a standard at my large parties. This recipe is adapted from the 50th Anniversary Issue of Gourmet Magazine, January 1991.

A 5 – 7 pound whole salmon, cleaned, rinsed and patted
   dry
¾ cup dry white wine
8 fresh basil leaves
3 fresh tarragon sprigs, plus additional for garnish
2 fresh rosemary sprigs
3 shallots, peeled and minced
2 lemon slices
3 sprigs of celery leaves

8 cups fish aspic (approximately) – recipe follows

Garnish – thin slices of turnip, cut with a cookie cutter to resemble a flower and reserved in cold water.
1 hard boiled egg yolk, mashed with 1 teaspoon butter as center of the turnip flower.

Preheat oven to 375 degrees. In a small saucepan combiner the wine, basil, 3 tarragon sprigs, rosemary, shallots, lemon and celery. Bring to a boil, then reduce to a simmer and continue to cook for 20 minutes or until mixture is reduced to about 3 tablespoons.
   Lay the salmon lengthwise on a piece of heavy-duty foil. The foil should be twice as long as the fish.
   Pick up the edges of the foil and pour the wine mixture over the salmon. Be sure to cover the tail well with sauce.
   Season the salmon with salt and fold the foil to enclose it, crimping the edges tightly to secure them.

Place the salmon on a large baking sheet or an inverted roasting pan in the middle of the oven and bake 50 minutes to 1 hour or until the flesh just flakes when touched with a fork.

When salmon is done, transfer foil package to a work surface, open the foil carefully. Using a small knife or fork, remove the skin from the top of the salmon, below the head, to the bottom of the salmon, above the tail – scraping away any brown flesh. Leave the head and tail intact.

Drain the liquid from the foil and using the foil as a guide, invert the fish onto a platter.

Remove the foil carefully. Remove the skin form the other side of the salmon in the same manner.

Chill the salmon, covered, for at least 6 hours or overnight.

Spoon a thin coat of cool, but liquid fish aspic over the salmon. Arrange the additional tarragon springs and reserved turnip flowers decoratively on the salmon. Place or pipe a small drop of the yolk mixture as the flower center.

Chill the aspic covered salmon for at least 2 hours and up to 6 hours. Surround salmon with chopped, chilled aspic. Serve with crackers and Sweet Mustard Dill Sauce.

Leftover salmon makes excellent salmon cakes.

Fish Aspic

6 cups bottled clam juice
2 cups white wine
6 envelopes of unflavored gelatin
The white and shells of 3 large eggs

In a large pan or stockpot place clam juice and wine. Sprinkle the gelatin over the liquid mixture.

In a mixing bowl beat egg whites until stiff. Crush egg shells. Add the beaten egg whites and crushed egg shells to wine and clam juice mixture. Do not stir them in until you begin the heating process.

Bring mixture slowly to a full boil over moderate heat, whisking constantly.

Remove pan form the heat and let stand for 30 minutes.

Strain the aspic through a fine sieve line with a dampened kitchen tea towel.

Let it cool. Place 2 cups of liquid in a measuring cup. This will be used to pour over the fish.

Place remaining liquid in a baking pan and refrigerate until it is solidified. This will be used to make the chopped aspic.

Once the aspic has solidified it may be cut into small cubes, diamonds or other decorative shapes.

The aspic may be made three days in advance and kept covered and chilled.

To liquefy the aspic, heat it in a saucepan over medium heat or microwave.

Sweet Mustard Dill Sauce
Makes about 1 cup

This sauce is excellent as a condiment for fish. It makes a great dipping sauce for vegetables, and makes an awesome Honey Mustard chicken. Simply smear the sauce over 1 chicken, cut up, and bake in a 350 degree oven for one hour.

½ cup honey-type mustard
½ cup mayonnaise
½ teaspoon dried dill leaves, or 1 ½ teaspoons chopped
    fresh dill leaves

Mix all ingredients together and refrigerate until ready to use. May be made 2 – 3 days in advance.

"Have nothing in your houses that you do not know to be useful, or believe to be beautiful."
- 19th century designer and poet William Morris

Gravlax
10 – 12 servings

Gravlax is so simple to make. It is an elegant appetizer and a special breakfast or brunch entrée. Serve as an appetizer with sweet mustard dill sauce. Offer crackers or small squares of black bread.

As a breakfast or brunch entrée, serve gravlax on bagels with cream cheese. Offer thinly sliced onions and capers as toppings.

One 2-pound salmon fillet, skin removed, halved
    lengthwise
3 tablespoons kosher salt
3 tablespoons sugar
12 or more black peppercorns, crushed
1 bunch fresh dill

Inspect salmon to make sure all the bones are removed. Place half of the salmon fillet, skin-side down on a large piece of plastic wrap or aluminum foil. In a small bowl, mix together salt, sugar and crushed peppercorns. Sprinkle over salmon fillet. Spread dill over salt/sugar mixture. Place the other half of salmon, skin side up, on top of the dill.

Wrap the salmon in plastic wrap or foil. Place in a pan and set a heavy board or cans on top of salmon. Refrigerate 48 – 72 hours, turning the salmon twice a day. The salt will draw juices out of the fish as it "cooks". The juices should remain in the sealed plastic wrap to marinate.

To serve, remove salmon from plastic wrap, scrape away dill and spices and pat dry. Slice the salmon in very thin diagonal slices.

"The salt cooks the salmon the same as heat."
- Chef Rick Moonen of Oceana Restaurant. Chef Moonen says the gravlax will keep up to two weeks in the refrigerator and will keep frozen *"indefinitely".*

Crab Cakes
Or
Salmon Cakes
Serves 6 as an appetizer
Serves 2 as a main course

The crab cakes may be made with Maryland Blue crab or the West Coast Dungeness crab. Both taste equally delicious, although the meat of the Blue crab holds together better than that of the Dungeness. All types of salmon work equally well.

10 ounces of crab*, picked over
2 handfuls of cornflakes, crumbled, about ½ cup
1 egg, lightly beaten
1 teaspoon celery seed
2 tablespoons mayonnaise
1 tablespoon chopped fresh parsley
Dash Worcestershire and/or dash hot pepper sauce
2 tablespoons butter

In a mixing bowl, lightly combine all ingredients, except butter. Shape mixture into four crab cakes, if using for entrée (2 per person). If making appetizers, make six smaller size crab cakes (1 per person).

In a large skillet, heat butter over medium heat. Sauté crab cakes until golden brown and cooked through, about 5 minutes per side.

Serve with a lemon wedge or roasted red bell pepper sauce.

A cooked 2 pound Dungeness crab provides approximately ½ pound crab meat.

*To make salmon cakes substitute cooked salmon for crab. Serve salmon cakes with a lemon wedge or lemon-herb mayonnaise.

Lemon-Herb Mayonnaise
Makes about 1 cup

This savory mayonnaise is a perfect compliment to all broiled, baked or grilled fish. It is equally good served with salmon cakes.

¾ cup mayonnaise
1 tablespoon fresh lemon juice
1 tablespoon prepared horseradish
2½ teaspoon chopped fresh thyme, or 1 teaspoon dried.

In a small bowl combine all ingredients. Season with salt and pepper to taste. Refrigerate until ready to use. May be made several days in advance.

Sun-Dried Tomato Canapés
Serves 6 – 8

These tasty little appetizers are easy to make and may be frozen ahead of time.

3 ounces sun-dried tomatoes (about 2 cups)
½ cup olive oil
2 tablespoon butter, melted
1 teaspoon Italian seasoning
1 large clove garlic, minced
9 slices coarse white bread (such as English Muffin Loaf)

Preheat oven to 350 degrees. Place tomatoes in a small bowl. Cover with boiling water. Let soak several minutes until soft. Drain water. Finely chop tomatoes.

In a medium bowl place chopped tomatoes, olive oil, melted butter, Italian seasoning and minced garlic. Stir to combine.

Remove crust from bread. Slice bread into finger-size pieces, about 1 x 3 inches.

Spread about 1 teaspoon of tomato mixture onto each bread slice. Place bread with tomato on baking sheet. The canapés may be covered and frozen at this point.

Bake approximately 10 minutes or until edges begin to brown. Baking will take longer if canapés are frozen.

Serve warm.

Vegetable Christmas Tree
Serves 10 – 12

This is an attractive addition to a Christmas buffet table. The only problem is guests often say "it is too pretty to eat."

2 bunches broccoli
1 small head cauliflower
1 pint basket cherry tomatoes

Favorite dip for raw vegetables

Line a large baking sheet with aluminum foil. Place the tray vertically and with a pencil draw the outline of a large triangle that will be the tree. Rinse broccoli and break the head into little florets. Place the florets on the foil in the outline to create the Christmas tree. Use a broccoli stem to make the tree trunk.

Clean the cauliflower and again break the head into little florets. Decorate the broccoli tree with cauliflower florets and cherry tomatoes, creating the effect of a tree with lights and ornaments. Place a bowl of your favorite dip next to the tree.

"At one time most of my friends could hear the bell, but years passed, it fell silent for all of them. Even Sarah found one Christmas that she could no loner hear its sweet sound. Though I've grown old, the bell still rings for me as it does for all who truly believe."
- **The Polar Express by Chris Van Allsburg.**

Shrimp Remoulade
Serves 6

Traditionally Shrimp Remoulade is served on a plate consisting of shredded Romaine lettuce , topped with shrimp, then covered with a remoulade sauce. Each guest receives an individual plate with lettuce, shrimp and sauce.

1 pound medium shrimp, cleaned, cooked and chilled
1 small head Romaine lettuce, shredded

For the Remoulade Sauce:
½ cup chopped celery
½ cup chopped green onions
½ cup olive oil
2 tablespoons Creole mustard (available in many grocery stores)
2 tablespoons ketchup
1 tablespoon white wine vinegar
1 tablespoon prepared horseradish
1 tablespoon paprika
1 tablespoon chopped fresh parsley
1 teaspoon Tabasco
1 teaspoon salt
Juice of ¼ lemon
1 clove garlic, minced

Place all ingredients for sauce in a blender. Process until all is combined and pureed. Refrigerate until ready to use. May be made several days in advance.

Lentil Soup
Serves 6 – 8

This is a hearty soup that needs only a salad and some crusty bread to make a complete and nutritional meal.

Lentils are my favorite legume with which to make soup in that they do not need to be soaked.

2 tablespoons olive oil
1 tablespoon butter
1 large onion, chopped, about 2 cups
1 cup chopped celery
1 cup chopped carrot
2 cloves garlic, minced
1 quart brown stock or beef bouillon
2 cups dried lentils (1 pound package), rinsed, picked-over
1 ham bone or ham hock
2 bay leaves
1 teaspoon salt
Freshly ground pepper, to taste

Melt butter and olive oil over medium heat in a large soup pot, approximately 6 quarts. Add onion, celery, carrot, and sauté until soft. Add garlic, stock, lentils, ham bone, bay leaves and seasonings. Bring to a boil. Reduce heat to a simmer and cover. Simmer on low heat for several hours, adding water as needed and stirring occasionally. Soup is done when lentils are soft.

Remove ham bone and bay leaves. Place soup through a food mill or puree in blender. Return to heat and serve.

Freezes well.

I often wonder if we ate more ham in the winter and thus more soup? Or, did Mother buy more ham so we could have more soup?

Chicken Stock
Makes 2 – 3 quarts

There are not words to describe the difference between canned chicken stock and homemade chicken stock. One must make their own stock to know the true greatness of recipes made with homemade stock.

This stock may be used as the base for soup or sauce. Once the stock is made, freeze in individual baggies of 1 cup each. This storage method makes recipe preparation easy. Stock will keep indefinitely in the freezer. It will keep several days in the refrigerator.

5-7 pounds of chicken meat and bones. Ask you butcher for chicken back bones to help reduce the cost of making stock

2 teaspoons salt
1 onion, peeled and quartered
2 carrots, scraped
2 stalks celery, with leaves
bouquet garni (a small bunch of parsley, several sprigs of
    thyme and a bay leaf, tied together with kitchen string)
several peppercorns

Place chicken and bones in a large stock pot. Add enough water so chicken is covered by at least one inch. Add remaining ingredients and bring to a boil. Skim off foam and reduce heat to a very low simmer. (Boiling will create a cloudy stock.)

Simmer for 5 – 8 hours. The cooking process may be stopped at any time. It usually takes me two, and often three, days to make stock. Refrigerate stock if cooking process is stopped for more than an hour or two.

The cooking process is complete when all of the flavor has been rendered out of the meat into the liquid. Drain stock. Discard chicken, vegetables and bones. Refrigerate liquid so that fat may be easily skimmed from the top.

When the stock has cooled, skim fat. Taste and adjust seasonings. If not using immediately, freeze in individual 1 cup containers.

*"If you have a friend worth loving,
Love him. Yes, and let him know
That you love him, ere life's evening
Tinge his brow with sunset glow:
Why should good words ne'er be said
Of a friend 'till he is dead?"*
- author unknown

Bean and Cabbage Soup
Serves 6

Another soul-soothing soup that needs only a salad and some bread to make a complete dinner. This soup does not taste like cabbage. Please try it – it is very good for you.

2 cups navy beans (1 pound package), rinsed, picked-over and soaked in water overnight.
1 head green cabbage, shredded - approximately 1 pound cabbage or 8 cups shredded.
¼ cup olive oil
1 large onion, chopped
2 cups chopped carrots
3 cups chicken stock
2 cups water
1 ham bone
2 cloves garlic, minced
2 bay leaves
1 teaspoon dried thyme leaves
1 teaspoon salt
Freshly ground pepper, to taste

In a large soup pot, approximately 6 quarts, heat oil over medium heat. Add onions and carrots, and sauté until soft. Add cabbage and cook until tender and wilted.

Add stock, water, beans, ham bone, garlic, bay leaves, thyme, salt and pepper. Bring to a boil, reduce heat and simmer until beans are cooked, about 2 hours.

Remove ham bone and bay leaves. Puree about half of the soup in a food processor or run through a food mill. Return to pot. Add more water or stock to reach desired consistency. Heat and serve.

The entire soup may be pureed if you like a smoother texture. Freezes well.

Split Pea soup
Serve 6

This recipe is adapted from one my mother-in-law gave me. She uses a crock pot and cooks the soup on low for about 6 hours. I prefer to make the soup on the stove and let it simmer for several hours. Both methods work well.

2 cups dried split peas, (1 pound package), rinsed, picked-over
1 tablespoon olive oil
1 tablespoon butter
1 medium onion, chopped
1 carrot, chopped
1 stalk celery, chopped
2 quarts cold water
1 ham bone or ham hock
1 bay leaf
2 teaspoons salt
Freshly ground pepper, to taste
Dash nutmeg
Milk

Soak the peas in water for several hours, if possible. If peas are not soaked, cooking time will be longer. Drain. In a large soup pot, approximately 6 quarts, melt butter and oil. Add the onions, carrots and celery, sauté over medium heat until soft.

Add the peas, the 2 quarts of water, ham bone, bay leaf, salt, pepper and nutmeg. Bring to a boil. Skim off any foam and reduce heat to a low simmer. Continue to simmer for several hours, stirring occasionally.

The soup should be very thick. If you like a smooth soup, remove the ham bone and bay leaf and puree the mixture. Return to pot. Add milk until desired consistency is achieved. (It is not necessary to add milk if you like the

soup very thick.) Heat and serve. Garnish with chopped
fresh parsley, if desired. Freezes well.

What is a split pea???? *"A split pea is actually a field
pea, less sweet than a garden pea. When dried this variety
of pea splits in half."*
-Anne William <u>La Varenne Pratique</u>

*"...beans are PC or should I say NC, meaning
nutritionally correct. Not only do they contain all the
right nutrients and proteins, which I shall refrain form
enumerating, but they are also 'all natural', cholesterol-
free, and are stylishly low in fat."*
- Julia Child

Green Gumbo
Serves 8

   Tradtionally a Lenten dish, legend has it that you would make as many friends as the number of different greens you put in this gumbo. I like making this dish because it tastes so good and is so good for you – but I also like making it when I think I might need a new friend or two. Adapted from The New Orleans Cookbook by Rima and Richard Collin.

Greens(as many of these as are available; a minimum of 5,
        7 or 8 is perfect)
1 bunch collard greens
1 bunch mustard greens
1 bunch turnip greens
1 bunch scallions
1 bunch parsley
1 bunch watercress
1 bunch spinach
1 bunch beet tops
1 bunch radish tops
1 small head green cabbage, stem removed
1 bunch carrot tops
1 bunch dandelion tops
1 bunch swiss chard

1/2 cup vegetable oil
2/3 cup flour
1 medium onion, chopped
2 quarts chicken stock
1 teaspoon salt
2 bay leaves, crushed
½ teaspoon dried thyme leaves
½ teaspoon dried marjoram
Pinch ground (cayenne) red pepper
Pinch allspice

Wash all greens thoroughly and trim off any tough stems or discolored leaves. Place the damp green in a large pot, add ⅓ cup water and turn heat to high. When liquid in the bottom of the pan begins to boil, cover the pan tightly, reduce heat to low and cook the greens for approximately 15 minutes or until just tender. Remove the pan from heat and drain the greens. Chop the cooked greens fine and set them aside.

In a heavy 3 to 4 quart saucepan or pot, heat oil over high heat. Reduce to low and gradually add the flour, stirring constantly. Cook over low heat, always stirring, until a golden brown roux develops, about the color of peanut butter. This will take a good 5 to 10 minutes. Once the desired color has been reached, add the onions and continue to cook and stir for several minutes. Next, gradually add the chicken stock, continuing to stir and cook with a wire whisk. When all the stock has been incorporated, add the remaining ingredients, including the greens. Bring mixture to a boil, then reduce to a simmer and continue to cook for another hour or so.

I like this dish just as it is – but the gumbo may be served over boiled rice, if desired. For those who like a spicy gumbo, pass hot pepper sauce when the dish is served.

Mixed Green Salad with Blue Cheese, Apple and Caramelized Nuts

Serves 2

Although this recipe is for 2, it may easily be doubled or tripled. There will be more caramelized nuts than is needed for the salad. I have found, however, that there are always sneaky fingers around – snatching up the nuts before they get to the salad.

Versatile Salad Dressing – recipe follows

½ cup nuts (pecans, walnuts or almond)
2 tablespoons sugar
1 apple peeled and sliced
1 ounce blue cheese, crumbled
Mixed salad greens, enough for 2

In a small pan place sugar and nuts. Turn heat on high and stir constantly until sugar melts and coats nuts. Remove nuts to wax paper to cool.

Place mixed greens on two salad plates. Top each salad with half an apple and half of the cheese. Drizzle with salad dressing. Top with caramelized nuts.

Versatile Salad Dressing
Makes about 2 cups

This salad dressing is good served over a wide variety of lettuces. It makes a great tossed salad and it is our favorite dressing for blue cheese, apple and caramelized nut salad.

½ cup sugar
1 teaspoon salt
1 teaspoon dry mustard
1 heaping teaspoon paprika
½ cup cider vinegar
½ cup vegetable or canola oil
½ cup olive oil

Mix dry ingredients. Whisk in vinegar and oil. Pour enough dressing over salad to that leaves are lightly coated when tossed.

Refrigerate remaining dressing. Dressing will keep several weeks in refrigerator.

The Baptism, First Communion, or Confirmation Brunch

As a new mother, I was overwhelmed at the thought of having "family" and friends for brunch after our first son's baptism. To begin with, I didn't want to invite all my husband's aunts – but Mother said I should. I then invited friends for support – I was convinced this would be a failure.

How could anyone get food and a house ready for a party Sunday morning?? – Especially when one is suffering from lack of sleep because the 6-month-old is still waking up 3 times a night. I cried, I panicked and I lost more sleep, but in hindsight, I'm glad I had the baptism brunch. It all turned out fine.

The secret to these after church affairs is to have just about everything done at least the day before. Make and freeze whatever is possible. Set the table and flowers the day (or two) ahead. Make sure the bar is set up the day before. Most importantly, keep things simple.

Nibble food (nuts, mints, popcorn, etc.)
Baked Ham
Banana Bread Pudding with Strawberry Sauce
Scrambled Eggs
Huge bowl or basket of fresh fruit
Cinnamon rolls and/or Bagels

Make banana bread pudding and strawberry sauce the day ahead. Assemble the bowl of fruit the day ahead.

The morning of the party, put the ham in the oven at a very low heat before departing for church.

When guests begin to arrive, cook the eggs, and heat cinnamon rolls and bread pudding.
Enroll lots of help putting everything on the table. Relax and enjoy.

Banana Bread Pudding with Strawberry Sauce
Serves 8 – 10

Traditionally a southern dessert, we like our bread pudding for breakfast, especially with a warm strawberry sauce. It is, however, very good for dessert and not bad for lunch, and come to think about it – it's excellent cold, any time of the day.

3½ cups milk
12 cups stale bread cubes, cut into 1½ - 2 inch cubes
¼ cup butter (1/2 stick)
2 ripe bananas, peeled and cut into ¼ inch slices
2/3 cup raisins
4 large eggs
½ cup firmly packed brown sugar
½ cup granulated sugar
1 teaspoon cinnamon
½ teaspoon vanilla extract
½ teaspoon fresh grated nutmeg
½ teaspoon salt
¼ teaspoon allspice

Butter a 3 – 4 quart casserole. Preheat oven to 350 degrees.

In a large saucepan, scald milk over medium heat. Remove from heat and add butter. Set aside until butter melts in hot milk.

In a large bowl place bread cubes, sliced bananas and raisins. Pour milk and butter mixture over bread and stir.

In a medium bowl beat eggs, add sugar, vanilla, cinnamon, nutmeg, salt and allspice. Beat until blended.

Stir egg mixture into bread and blend. Pour mixture into casserole. Bake for about 1 hour or until knife inserted into center comes out clean. Serve warm or chilled with strawberry sauce.

Strawberry Sauce
Makes about 2 cups

1 pound frozen strawberries
½ cup sugar
1 tablespoon raspberry liquor

In a medium sauce pan place strawberries to defrost. Mash berries and add sugar. Bring mixture to a boil and cook about 5 minutes or until sauce begins to thicken. Remove from heat. Skim off any foam. Stir in liquor.

Serve with bread pudding, ice cream, angel food cake, meringues, or chocolate torte.

"Eating is fun, and cooking is fun, and to hell with all the calories and balanced meals! Let us again sit around big, comfortable tables and enjoy our meals ...Good food is best at home, and bad food is bad everywhere. Good food is fun, and bad food is a menace."
- Bill Rhode, The Solace of Food by Robert Clark

Mom's Egg and Cheese Breakfast Soufflé
Serves 4

More of an egg and cheese casserole than a true soufflé, this breakfast dish is easy to make, fail proof, and always delicious. The soufflé is especially suited for house guests or for mornings when you know you are not going to be in the mood to cook. It must be assembled the day ahead and kept refrigerated overnight.

It is better to make two soufflés than to try and double the recipe in a larger baking dish.

9 slices of white bread (with crust), cut into 1 inch strips
½ pound Velveeta cheese, cut in chunks
¼ pound butter (1 stick)
4 eggs
2 cups milk
Dash salt

Grease a 1 ½ quart casserole. In the top of a double boiler, place cheese and butter. Cook and stir over medium heat until butter and cheese are melted.

To assemble the soufflé , place ⅓ of the bread strips on the bottom of the casserole dish. Spoon ⅓ of cheese and butter mixture over the bread. Repeat until you have three layers. Pour egg and milk mixture over the bread and cheese. Cover and refrigerate overnight.

Preheat oven to 325 degrees. Place covered casserole in oven and bake for 45 minutes. Remove cover and continue to bake an additional 15 minutes or until set.

Donut Making on Martin Luther King's Birthday

Makes 18 donuts or 3 dozen donut holes

Martin Luther King's birthday is one holiday I never seem to know what to do with the children. Husbands are usually working and the weather is almost guaranteed to be miserable. So I have found it is great day to make donuts. There is nothing better than a fresh, warm, homemade donut, coated with powdered sugar. It is a true culinary experience.

So let each of the kids invite a friend to help. Make the dough the night before. Have plenty of orange juice and milk on hand, and be prepared for a big mess in the kitchen.

It will be a wonderful, fun-filled morning - one that your children will want to repeat sooner than you are ready.

This is what memories are made of:

2 cups flour
2 teaspoons baking powder
¼ teaspoon nutmeg
½ teaspoon salt
1 egg, beaten
½ cup milk
½ cup sugar
1 tablespoon melted butter or salad oil

Vegetable or canola oil for frying

Cookie cutter to make donuts

For the Toppings – For powdered sugar donuts, place approximately 2 cups of powdered sugar in a brown paper bag. For cinnamon sugar donuts, place 1 cup sugar and 2 teaspoons cinnamon in a brown paper bag. For glazed donuts, place 2 cups of powdered sugar with 1 teaspoon vanilla in a small bowl, add ⅓ cup water and pinch of salt – whisk until glaze is smooth.

To Make Donuts:

Sift flour, baking powder, salt, and nutmeg together and place in a large mixing bowl. In a separate bowl whisk together the egg, milk, sugar and butter – add to flour mixture – combine and kneed to make a smooth dough, adding more flour as necessary to make dough firm enough to handle but keeping as soft as possible. About ½ to 1 cup more flour will be needed.

Chill about one hour. Dough may be kept in refrigerator for a day if covered and tightly wrapped.

When you are ready to make donuts, put a third of the mixture on a floured board, knead slightly, pat and roll out to ⅓ inch thick. With a donut cutter, cut out donuts. (I use a wreath cookie cutter. My children actually prefer donut holes – made simply with a 1-inch circle cookie cutter.)

To fry: Heat vegetable oil in a deep fryer or skillet to 360 degrees. Donuts will absorb fat if the oil is too cool, and will brown before they are done in the center if the oil is too hot.

Lower donuts, three or four at a time, into oil. When brown on one side, turn and brown the other side. Lift from oil with fork or tongs and place on a paper plate or towel to drain – then carefully place the hot donut in glazing bowl or sugar filled bag. Gently shake bag until donut is well coated. After glazing, place donut on a wire rack to cool and dry. Repeat procedure until all the dough is used.

This recipe doubles well. Be sure to make enough donuts to send a plate-full home with each of your guests, Oh, and don't forget leftovers for the next morning.

Winter II

Entrees

Side Dishes

Christmas Dinner
One of the best presents you can give the family

Christmas dinner is a meal to which we all look forward; good food shared with family and friends after a wonderful day of gift, hug, and kiss giving. It is a meal that is remembered and talked about for years to come.

All this is very good except when it is your turn to cook the Christmas dinner. You've been up since 5 am with the children, the house is a wreck with toys and wrapping paper, and ten relatives are coming for a spectacular meal in several hours. It is enough to overwhelm the most confident of chefs.

But Christmas dinner should not be a reason to panic. With a little planning and a little beforehand cooking, an elegant meal can be presented with little or no stress and should provide a lot of enjoyment and satisfaction.

P.S. Christmas Day is not a good time to try a new recipe. If you want to serve something new, experiment several weeks in advance. Test the recipe to make sure it is easy and delicious.

Christmas Dinner for 15

Gravlax
Apples and Pears with Cheese

Standing Rib Roast
Swiss Chard Timbales
Scalloped Potatoes
Caesar Salad
Dinner Rolls

Christmas Cake

Game Plan:

A week or two in advance, bake and freeze the cake. Three days in advance make the gravlax. The timbales may be made 24 hours ahead. Set the tables at least one day in advance.

On Christmas Day, defrost and ice the cake. Make the potatoes in the morning and refrigerate until time to bake. Determine cooking and finishing time for meat and potatoes. Clean the lettuce and make the salad dressing. Slice the fruit and bring out the gravlax when the guests arrive.

Standing Rib Roast

A standing rib roast is one of the most delicious and easiest entrees one can serve at a large gathering. It is perfect for a big buffet, a family gathering, or a grand dinner party.

Selection:
A full rib roast has seven ribs to a side. The old standard for determining a serving was 1 rib per 2 people. However, under current guidelines, this is way too much beef per person. I have found a 5-rib roast, approximately 9-10 pounds, will serve 12 people. A 6-rib roast will serve 14 with leftovers.

When purchasing beef always ask for the loin end or the small end. This will give you the best cut of beef. To make matters confusing, the small end begins with the largest ribs and the most meat. If the butcher is not available and you are selecting the beef by yourself, look for the large ribs with almost all beef, the smaller ribs or the "large end" will have more fat.

Although boneless rib roast is an option, cooking beef with the ribs helps retain the juices and reduces shrinkage. To make carving easier, have the butcher cut the ribs from the beef and then tie them back together.

Roasting:
To calculate roasting time, figure 18-20 minutes per pound for medium-rare. To ensure the meat is cooked to the desired stage always use a meat thermometer.
Rare – Internal temperature should register at 125°.
Medium – Internal temperature should register at 140°.
Well Done – Internal temperature should register at 160°.

Always make sure the meat is brought to room temperature before beginning the cooking process. Season the beef with salt and pepper and small slivers of garlic tucked in the outer layer of fat.

Preheat the oven to 450 degrees. Roast the beef in the lower third of the oven.

Place the roast in the 450 degree oven for 15 minutes to produce crisp crust, then lower heat to 350 degrees to finish. If the roast is larger than 8 pounds reduce the temperature to 325 degrees after the initial high heat.

The final step to ensure a delicious roast is to let the beef "rest" for 20-30 minutes after being removed from the oven. "Tent" the roast with foil while it rests to keep the meat warm. Be sure to include the resting time when calculating what time you will serve the meal. Large roasts will continue to cook for up to 10 minutes after being removed from the oven.

Accompaniments:

One of our favorite accompaniments for roast beef is freshly grated horseradish. Serve this in a bowl and pass, letting guests determine if they would like a pinch or a bunch of this pungent root vegetable. Another favorite is to sere the beef 'au jus' (with its juice). Simply skim the fat off the drippings in the pan. Add 1-2 cups beef stock or a combination of beef stock and red wine to the drippings. Place the pan over high heat. Bring to a boil, scrape the drippings off the bottom and stir. Continue to boil until mixture is reduced by half. Season with salt and pepper and serve over beef.

"Always use freshly ground pepper. It does make a big difference."
- **Jacque Peppin**

Beef Tenderloin
Serves 8-10

One 3-4 pound beef tenderloin
2 tablespoons canola oil
Salt and pepper
½ cup red wine

Trim any fat from the tenderloin. Rub with about 1 teaspoon oil and season with salt and pepper. Preheat oven to 425 degrees.

Place remaining oil in a heavy roasting pan. Place roasting pan on stove top. Over medium-high heat, brown tenderloin in oil on all sides. Remove tenderloin and pour out oil. Add wine to the hot roasting pan and deglaze by stirring and scraping-up browned pieces in pan. Return tenderloin to roasting pan with wine. Spoon several teaspoons of wine over the beef.

Place tenderloin in oven and roast for 35-45 minutes, or until meat thermometer registers at 125 degrees for rare or 140 degrees for medium-well.

Let meat rest, covered, for at least ten minutes before carving. Pan drippings may be spooned over the beef if desired.

When roasting at high temperatures it is import to have a clean oven. Unclean ovens will begin to smoke when the internal oven reaches 400 degrees or higher. There are few things more embarrassing than the smoke detector going off while you are trying to cook a gourmet meal for friends.

Scalloped Potatoes
Serves 6

1½ pounds Russet Potatoes (about 3 medium), peeled,
  sliced thinly, 1/8-1/4 inch thick
1½ cups cheddar cheese, about 5 ounces*
Salt and pepper
¾ cup butter milk

Preheat oven to 375 degrees. Grease a 1½ quart
casserole dish. Divide potatoes and cheese into thirds.

Line the bottom of the casserole dish with ⅓ of the
potatoes. Sprinkle lightly with salt and pepper. Top with ⅓
of the shredded cheese. Repeat this procedure two more
times, creating three layers each of potatoes and cheese.
Pour buttermilk over all. Potatoes may be made ahead up to
this point. Cover and refrigerate until ready to bake.

Bake covered casserole for 1½ hours. Uncover and
continue to bake for about 30 minutes or until potatoes are
soft when pierced with a fork.

Let stand several minutes before serving. Excellent
with roast pork, chicken, or beef. Also delicious served at
breakfast or brunch with ham or sausage.

*** Try substituting goat cheese for cheddar cheese or use
5 ounces of any of your favorite cheeses.**

Swiss Chard Timbales
Serves 6

Timbales are a great party vegetable. Baked in individual molds, they make an attractive presentation and best of all they can be made hours in advance. Substitute spinach for the swiss chard if you like, or try 2½-3 cups cooked vegetable of your choice in place of the chard.

6 1-cup molds or ramekins, or a 1½ quart soufflé mold
2 bunches of swiss chard, about 1½ pounds
1 tablespoon olive oil
½ cup finely minced onion
2/3 cup bread crumbs
¼ cup grated Parmesan cheese
5 eggs
1 cup milk brought to a boil with 4 tablespoons butter
¼ teaspoon salt
Pinch of nutmeg
Freshly ground pepper to taste

Preheat oven to 325 degrees. Heat water which will be poured into a pan where the timbales will bake. Grease the molds. Rinse and clean the chard, removing stems.

Bring a large pot of boiling water to a boil. Add chard, pushing leaves under water with a long handled spoon until leaves wilt. Continue to cook for an additional 2-3 minutes. Drain chard in a colander and let cool.

In a small saucepan, heat olive oil, add onions and sauté until soft. In a large mixing bowl, place sautéed onions, bread crumbs, and cheese. Stir to combine. Whisk in eggs one at a time, beating after each addition. Bring milk and butter to boiling point in the microwave or a small saucepan. Pour hot milk in a thin stream into egg mixture, stirring constantly. Add salt, pepper, and nutmeg.

Squeeze dry chard and chop. Fold chard into egg and milk mixture. Pour into molds. Place molds in a large baking pan. Add boiling water to pan until the water reaches half way up the outside of the molds. Place the pan in the lower third of the oven and bake for 35-40 minutes. Timbales are done when a knife plunged through the center comes out clean.

Remove molds from water and allow to settle for 5 minutes. Run a knife around the edge of the timbale and reverse on a serving platter.

If timbales are not to be served immediately, they may be unmolded and microwaved later, or they may be left in the pan of hot water and when ready, reheat the water on stove top until timbales are warm. Unmold and serve.

Timbale: This word is used in various senses. Originally, a timbale was a small metal drinking goblet, such timbales are now usually made of silver or silver plate and are purely decorative, being given to babies at birth or as christening presents.

Today, however, the word is applied chiefly to a plain, round high-sided mould and the preparation cooked in it.

- **<u>Larousse Gastronomique</u>**

Winter Vegetables with Horseradish Butter
Serves 8

These vegetables not only taste good together, but they make a pretty, colorful presentation.

2 pounds red potatoes, clean, skin-on, cut into pieces about
    the size of brussel sprouts
1 pound brussel sprouts
½ pound carrots, peeled, cut into 1 inch pieces
½ pound parsnips, cut into 1 inch pieces

Clean and cut potatoes. Clean brussel sprouts by rinsing, cutting off stems, then cut an x in the bottom of each for even cooking.

Place all cleaned and cut vegetables in a large bowl of ice water until ready to cook. The vegetables may sit in the water for several hours.

To cook vegetables, drain from water, place all in a steamer and cook for about 10 minutes or until tender.

Vegetables may be served plain or with Horseradish Butter.

Horseradish Butter

4 tablespoons butter
1 tablespoon prepared horseradish, drained
1 tablespoon cider vinegar

In a saucepan, melt butter. Stir in horseradish and vinegar. Pour over vegetables or place in a small sauce boat and pass with vegetables.

"A good host and hostess are well-prepared to see to the needs of their guests, having carefully planned for their comfort and entertainment."
- Emily L. Post

A Southern New Year's Day Dinner

Everyone wants to get the New Year off to a good start, and what better way to do it than by eating foods that will bring you good luck, money and good health? My mother always fixed roast pork, sauerkraut, and mashed potatoes on New Year's Day. She said it was a German custom that could bring you wealth in the coming year. We never got rich, but I always enjoyed the pork and sauerkraut.

While living in Atlanta, Ga., our neighbors invited us to a Southern New Year's Day dinner. Tricia Johnson explained that the traditional food was supposed to bring you good luck and health in the coming year. It was a wonderful meal, and we toast the South, our health, and good fortune every New Year's Day that we enjoy this delicious 'down-home' food.

Pulled Pork with Georgia Bar-B-Que Sauce
Black-eyed peas
Collards
Applesauce
Buttermilk Biscuits
Lemon Chess Pie

This meal is simple to prepare, but the food does need a long time cooking. It is a great meal to make while watching football games or relaxing in front of a fire. The pork cooks slowly in an oven for 5 – 6 hours. The sauce may be made a week or two in advance and kept refrigerated.

The black-eye peas also need to simmer several hours. The collards cook for an hour or more.

The applesauce may be made in an hour, but is best if it is also cooked slowly for several hours.

The pie may be made a day ahead. The only last minute preparation is baking the biscuits.

Black-eyed Peas
Serves 8 – 10

Black-eyed peas are actually beans and are cooked accordingly. They must be soaked in water overnight before cooking.

Eating black-eyed peas on New Year's Day will bring good luck in the coming year, according to Southern lore.

1 pound black-eyed peas, rinsed, picked-over and soaked in
    water overnight
1 ham bone or ham hock
1 medium onion, chopped
½ cup chopped celery
1 teaspoon dried thyme
1 teaspoon salt

In a large stock pot, place black-eyed peas that have been soaked, ham bone or hock, chopped onion, celery, thyme and salt. Cover with 6 cups of water. Bring to a boil. Reduce heat to a simmer and continue to cook, covered, for several hours or until black-eyed peas are soft. Drain and serve.

Black-eyed peas also cook well in a crockpot. They need 3 to 4 hours of cooking time on high.

Collard Greens
Serves 6 – 8

Collard greens are a type of cabbage, possibly one of the oldest forms, according to Anne Willan. The dark green leaves are much sturdier then those of cabbage and stand up well to long cooking. Collard greens are an excellent choice of fresh vegetables in the winter.

3 – 4 pounds of collard greens
1 ham bone or ham hock

Rinse greens and remove stems. Place ham bone or hock in a large pot. Add several inches of water and bring to a boil. Add collard greens, pushing down with a long handle spoon until greens wilt.

Reduce heat to a simmer. Cover and continue to cook on low for about an hour or until greens are tender.

Drain and serve with vinegar, if desired. Lots of Southerners like their vinegar steeped with a hot chili pepper before serving on collards.

A New Year's Wish
(from an old Irish toast)
May you have:
Enough happiness to keep you sweet.
Enough trials to keep you strong.
Enough sorrow to keep you human.
Enough hope to keep you happy.
Enough failure to keep you humble.
Enough success to keep you eager.
Enough friends to give you comfort.
Enough wealth to meet your needs.
Enough enthusiasm to look forward.
Enough faith to banish depression.
Enough determination to make today better than yesterday.

Buttermilk Biscuits
Makes 12 – 18 biscuits

2 cups flour
4 teaspoons baking powder
1 tablespoon sugar
¼ teaspoon salt
3 tablespoons butter
1 – 2 cups buttermilk

Preheat oven to 450 degrees. Grease two 8-inch round cake pans. In a medium mixing bowl, combine flour, baking powder, sugar and salt. Cut in butter with pastry cutter or two knives and blend until mixture resemble a course meal. Alternatively, a food processor may be used.

Slowly add 1 cup buttermilk, stirring. Add additional buttermilk until mixture forms a ball. Flour your hands and roll and pat dough into 2 – 3 inch biscuits. Place biscuits in cake pan. Biscuits should just touch each other. For golden brown biscuits brush tops with a little extra buttermilk. Bake for 15 minutes or until golden brown.

Buttermilk: Natural buttermilk is the liquid whey left behind when milk has been churned and the fat extracted as butter. Commercial buttermilk is made by adding a bacterial culture to low-fat or skim milk. In breads, pancakes and biscuits, buttermilk not only gives flavor, but its acid reacts with the baking soda, releasing gas that raises the dough.

Is it a Roll, a Biscuit or a Muffin?????

According to Randon House Dictionary:

Roll – *n.* a small cake of bread, often rolled or doubled on itself before baking.

Biscuit –*n.* a kind of bread in small cakes, raised with baking powder or soda.

Muffin –*n.* a small cup-shaped bread, usually eaten hot with butter.

Baked Ham

When purchasing a baked ham it is best to choose the butt portion rather than the shank. There is more meat in proportion to bone in the ham butt than there is in the ham shank.

The secret to a good ham is slow cooking. Remember most hams are already cooked, all you are doing is reheating. (Check labeling on ham – some hams are "partially" cooked and may require more baking time.)

Cooking the meat too fast at too high a temperature will produce a dry, chewy, ham.

For best results bake the ham in a 275 degree oven at 10 minutes per pound. Place the ham on a rack in the lower third portion of the oven.

If you are not in a hurry, you may reduce the heat to 250 degrees and figure about 15 minutes per pound.

Before baking, the ham may be studded with whole cloves. Others prefer to smear a mixture of honey and mustard on the ham. Both methods work well.

Unlike other meats, ham does not need to rest before carving.

"So many people walk around with a meaningless life. They are half-asleep, even when they're busy doing things they think are important. This is because they are chasing the wrong things. The way you get meaning into your life is to devote yourself to loving others, devote yourself to your community around you, and devote yourself to creating something that gives you purpose and meaning."
- Tuesdays with Morrie, by Mitch Albom

Succotash
Serves 4

This side dish makes excellent use of frozen vegetables. I always recommend using fresh vegetables in season. However, during the winter months the selection of fresh produce from the United States is limited.

January and February are the perfect time to sample the frozen vegetable section at your grocery. A little spice or flavoring goes a long way to bring frozen vegetables back to life. Try simmering your frozen vegetables in chicken stock or add a dash of your favorite seasoning.

Winter's not so bad after all.

1 cup frozen lima beans
1 cup frozen corn kernels
½ cup chopped frozen bell peppers
1 tablespoon butter
½ cup chicken stock
½ teaspoon Creole or Cajun seasoning

In a medium skillet, heat the butter. Add the frozen vegetables and sauté several minutes. Add chicken stock and seasonings. Bring mixture to a boil, then reduce to a simmer. Continue to simmer vegetables until liquid is almost evaporated.

Serve succotash with ham, pork or chicken.

Succotash is an American Indian dish made of corn kernels and lima beans.

Don't you just love to say that word?

Ham, Cheese and Roasted Red Bell Pepper Casserole
Serves 4- 6

A wonderful recipe for leftover ham.

½ pound pasta, cooked (penne, bow ties or spaghetti broken into 1-inch pieces)
1 large red bell pepper, roasted, charred, skin and seeds removed, roughly chopped.
¼ pound Monterey Jack Cheese, grated, about 1 cup
2 cups cooked ham, cut into ½ inch cubes
1 medium onion, chopped, about 1 cup
2 tablespoons olive oil
1 tablespoon butter
3 tablespoons flour
2 cups chicken stock
¼ cup white wine
¼ cup milk
1 tablespoon chopped fresh sage leaves
⅓ cup grated Parmesan cheese

Preheat oven to 350 degrees. Cook pasta, drain and set aside. Prepare bell pepper and set aside.

Heat olive oil and butter in a large saucepan. Add onions and sauté over medium heat until soft. Do not brown. Add flour and continue to cook and stir for one minute. Add stock, and continue to stir until mixture comes to a boil and begins to thicken. Reduce heat and add wine, milk and sage. Remove from heat. Add salt and pepper to taste.

Stir in cheese, ham, bell pepper, and pasta. Pour into a 2 quart baking dish. Top with Parmesan cheese. (Casserole may be prepared ahead to this point. Cover and refrigerate up to 24 hours before baking.)

Bake, uncovered, for approximately 40 minutes or until mixture begins to bubble and the top browns.

An After Holiday Family Meal
with
Grilled Chicken Sandwiches

Bread Sticks and Olives
Split Pea Soup
Grilled Chicken Sandwiches

After all the fancy and rich food of the holidays, it is always nice to return to simple, basic meals. Split pea soup is about as simple as it gets, and it is such as nice way to use the ham bone from Christmas Eve.

Grilled Chicken Sandwiches

Allow approximately one boneless, skinless chicken breast per person. Place breast between sheets of plastic wrap and pound until breasts are ½ inch or less thick. If breast is too large for a roll, cut in half. Wipe dry with paper towel then salt and pepper each breast. Sauté each breast in a pan with oil until brown on both sides and done.

Serve chicken on a toasted roll with cheese. To make the roll, place open hamburger rolls on a cookie sheet. Put cheese on one side of the roll. Place cookie sheet in broiler and broil until cheese melts and roll is brown. This will only take a minute or so.

If you have the time, this sandwich is also good with sautéed onions.

Every man should eat and drink and enjoy the fruits of all his labor.
-   Ecclesiastics 5:18

Plain Ol' Chili
Serves 8-10

This recipe makes a lot of chili. I like it this way because I serve our family half of the recipe for dinner one night and freeze the other half for an evening where there is no time for cooking. However, if you only want to make a small batch, this recipe easily divides in half.

I wish I could think of something better to eat with chili than coleslaw and cornbread, but I can't.

2 pounds ground beef
2 medium onions, chopped
4, 15½ -ounce cans of kidney beans, partially drained
2, 28-ounce cans of tomatoes
2, 8-ounce cans of tomato sauce
6 tablespoons chili powder
4 tablespoons cider vinegar
2 teaspoons salt
Freshly ground pepper to taste

Sauté chopped onions and ground beef in a large kettle over medium heat until beef is brown. Drain the fat. Add kidney beans, tomatoes with liquid, tomato sauce, chili powder, vinegar, salt, and pepper. Bring mixture to a boil. Reduce heat to a simmer and continue to cook for at least 20 minutes. Stir occasionally.

Offer toppings such as grated cheddar cheese, chopped onions, sour cream, chopped cilantro, or sliced black olives when you serve chili. May be made the day ahead and also freezes well.

"It is as really a part of education to be able to blacken a stove, scour a tin, or prepare a tempting meal of wholesome food, as it is to be able to solve a problem in geometry, to learn a foreign language, to teach a school..."
- **Mary Johnson Lincoln, The Boston School Kitchen Text Book, 1884**

Texas Cowboy Chili
Serves 4

I read somewhere that the cowboys of Texas did not put beans in their chili, I don't know if this is true or not, but my kids like this version of chili best. It probably has something to do with the name.

Try purchasing whole dried red chilies and grinding them yourself in a coffee grinder or blender. I think you will be surprised at the difference it makes in the taste of chili. However, 3 tablespoons of regular chili powder may be substituted for the ground chilies, oregano, and cumin.

1 tablespoon olive oil
1 pound chuck roast or sirloin cut into bite-sized cubes, or 1
    pound ground beef
1 large onion, chopped
2 tablespoons flour
2½ cups beef broth
1, 28-ounce can tomatoes, chopped with liquid
1 tablespoon tomato paste
2 cloves garlic, chopped
1 tablespoon ground dried red chilies (or to taste)*
1 teaspoon ground cumin
½ teaspoon ground oregano
1 teaspoon salt
Ground pepper to taste

In a stockpot heat oil. Add beef and sauté until brown. Transfer beef to a platter. Over medium heat, add onions and sauté until soft. Stir in flour and continue to cook and stir for about 1 minute.

Add beef stock and stir until mixture comes to a boil and begins to thicken. Reduce heat to a simmer and add tomatoes, tomato paste, beef, garlic, and spices. Continue to simmer for 1-2 hours, stirring occasionally.

Offer traditional toppings with chili. See Plain Ol' Chili. May be made the day ahead and reheated. Freezes well.

* This makes for a spicy chili. To reduce heat, cut the amount of dried chilies in half

This is a great recipe for left-over steak or roast beef.

Chicken Chili
Serves 6

This is a great award-winning chili recipe, but remember to remove the seeds from the jalapenos or it will become a fire house chili recipe.

4 cups cooked chicken or turkey cut into bite-size pieces.
    (One 3-pound chicken, cooked, skinned, boned, and
    cut up.)
2 tablespoons olive oil
1 large onion, peeled and chopped
1 cup chopped green bell pepper
3 small jalapeno peppers, seeded and diced (or to taste)
3 cloves of garlic, peeled and minced
1, 28-ounce can tomatoes, chopped with liquid
1 cup chicken broth
2, 15½ -ounce cans kidney beans, partially drained
1 tablespoon Worcestershire sauce
1 tablespoon Dijon mustard
2 tablespoons chili powder
2 teaspoons ground cumin
½ teaspoon dried oregano
¼ teaspoon ground red pepper
1 teaspoon salt
Ground pepper to taste

Cut cooked chicken in to bite-size pieces. Set aside.

In a large pot, heat oil over medium-high heat. Add chopped onions and both peppers. Sauté until soft. Stir in garlic. Add tomatoes and chicken broth. Bring mixture to a boil. Reduce to a simmer and add chicken and kidney beans. Stir in Worcestershire sauce, Dijon mustard, chili powder, cumin, oregano, red pepper, salt and pepper. Bring mixture back to a simmer and continue to cook for 20-30 minutes.

Corn Bread
Serves 6

We like to bake our cornbread in a cast-iron skillet, just like the Indians, pilgrims, and cowboys! (At least we like to think that's what they did.) A modern day baking pan works just as well. It's just not as much fun.

¼ cup butter or margarine
1 cup cornmeal
1 cup flour
4 tablespoons sugar
4 tablespoons baking powder
½ teaspoon salt
1 cup milk
1 egg beaten

Preheat oven to 400 degrees. Place the butter or margarine in a 9-inch cast-iron skillet or an 8x8 inch baking pan. Place the pan in the oven to melt the butter or margarine.

In a medium mixing bowl mix the cornmeal, flour, sugar, baking powder, and salt. Stir in milk and egg. When the butter has melted, remove pan from oven. Stir melted shortening into cornmeal mixture. Spoon mixture into hot baking pan.

Place in oven and bake 12-15 minutes or until golden brown. Serve warm.

Substitutions

Baking Powder: 1 teaspoon = ¼ teaspoon baking soda + ½ teaspoon cream of tartar

Buttermilk: 1 cup = 1 cup yogurt

Chocolate: 1 ounce = 3 tablespoons cocoa + 1 tablespoon butter

Cornstarch: 1 tablespoon = 2 tablespoons flour (as thickening)

Honey: 1 cup = 1 ¼ cup sugar + ¼ cup liquid

Tomato Sauce: 2 cups = ¾ cup tomato paste + 1 cup water

Cioppino
Serves 6

This famous California fish stew is wonderful if made correctly. There are, however way too many over-cooked, flavorless versions sold in San Francisco tourist restaurants. Cioppino is not inexpensive to make and be wary of any cheap version.

The first secret to making a good Cioppino is to ensure the seafood is fresh. The California Dungeness Crab is in season from December to February, which makes that the best time to make cioppino.

The second secret to making a good Cioppino is the slow simmering of the sauce, adding the seafood only at the end of cooking, and serving the dish when the seafood is just done.

1 Dungeness Crab, cooked, cleaned, and cracked
2 pounds clams, about 2 dozen
½ pound shrimp, rinsed and shelled
1 pound fish fillet, such as snapper, cod, or bass
¼ cup olive oil
1 onion chopped
½ cup chopped green bell pepper
2 cloves garlic, minced
3, 14-ounce cans tomatoes, chopped with liquid
2 tablespoons tomato paste
2 cups red wine
½ teaspoon crushed red pepper
2 bay leaves
1 teaspoon dried basil
1 teaspoon dried oregano
1 teaspoon dried thyme
Chopped fresh parsley as a garnish, optional

Soak the clams in cold water. Cut fish into bite-size pieces. Shell shrimp. Pick crab from cleaned and cracked shell and set aside. Crab claws may be added to the stew, whole, for a dramatic presentation or crab can be picked from the claws.

In a large saucepan, heat oil over medium heat. Add onions, bell peppers, and garlic. Simmer until soft. Add remaining ingredients, except seafood. Bring to a boil, reduce heat to a simmer and continue to cook on low for 20-30 minutes or until mixture reduces and begins to thicken. Season with salt and pepper to taste. The stew may be made several hours in advance up to this point. Keep seafood refrigerated until ready to cook.

Bring wine and tomato mixture back to a boil and add seafood. Cover and reduce heat to medium and cook 5-7 minutes or until fish is tender, shrimp turns pink, and clams open. Discard any clams that have not opened.

Ladle into bowls, sprinkle with chopped parsley, if desired.

"Serve with plenty of red wine and good bread."
- **James Beard**

Cornish Game Hens with Fruit Stuffing
Serves 3-6

Cornish Game Hens are very similar to chicken, smaller, and perhaps a little more tasty. They are, however, definitely cuter than a chicken and as such are a good choice for entertaining and special occasions.

One-half a bird is usually an adequate serving. If you have hearty eaters you might want to consider serving each guest a whole bird.

The birds may be stuffed and cooked earlier in the day and reheated in a 350 degree oven for 35 minutes. (Do not stuff the bird earlier in the day unless you are planning to cook then.)

The stuffing is delicious. This recipe makes enough to stuff each bird and there will be stuffing to fill a quart casserole.

3 Cornish Game Hens, cleaned, rinsed, patted dry
2 cups chicken stock
1 cup long grain rice
2 tablespoons butter
1 small onion, peeled and diced, about ½ cup
2 ribs celery, cleaned and diced
2 cooking apples, peeled, cored, diced
1 pear, peeled, cored, diced
⅓ cup chopped, dried apricots
1 teaspoon salt
¼ teaspoon thyme leaves
Freshly ground pepper
3 tablespoons olive oil
½ cup white wine

Preheat oven to 400 degrees. Clean the birds and let them sit at room temperature while the stuffing is prepared.

In a quart saucepan, bring the chicken stock and rice to a boil. Stir, reduce heat to low and cover. Continue to cook for 15 – 20 minutes or until rice is tender and the liquid is absorbed.

While the rice is cooking, melt the butter in a small pan. Add the diced onions and celery. Saute over medium heat until soft.

When the rice is done cooking remove from heat. Stir in celery/onion mixture. Add apples, pear and apricots.

Salt and pepper the inside of the birds. Fill each cavity with stuffing. Place leftover stuffing in a greased casserole. Heat stuffing for 15 minutes at 350 degree before serving.

Tie each hen's legs together with kitchen string. Tuck wings under bird. Place in roasting pan. Season outside with salt and pepper. Rub olive oil over each bird. Pour wine over all.

Place hens in a 400 degree oven and roast for 30 minutes. Reduce heat to 350 degrees. Baste with pan juices. Continue to cook for an additional 40 minutes. Baste every 15 – 20 minutes during cooking.

Remove hens from oven. Cover with foil and let stand 15 minutes before serving*

The hens may be brought to the table whole on a platter for presentation. They are easily cut in half with a knife. Or, they may be cut before serving. The stuffing should divide neatly with half remaining in each cavity.

*If the birds have been cooked earlier in the day, remove them from refrigerator and bring to room temperature. Preheat oven to 350 degrees and bake for 35 minutes. They do not need to rest after being warmed.

SUBSTITUTE !!! Never pass up a recipe because you don't like one ingredient. Substitute! If you don't like apricots, try dried cranberries. If you don't have pears, just use apples. Some of my best recipes have come from days when I thought I had an ingredient and I didn't – so I either had to leave it out or try something else. Just go for it, it will probably be great.

A Super Superbowl Party

The Superbowl is a great excuse for a party – whether it just be immediate family or a group of friends and family. We like to keep the menu limited to finger food, no silverware with which to fuss. And the atmosphere – about as casual as it can get. We usually hold our party in the kids' playroom. It's not beautiful, but it's different and it's fun – and there are plenty of games to play when the one on television gets boring.

Peanuts
Popcorn
Steamed shrimp (optional)

Parmesan Mustard Chicken Wings
Baked Potato Skins
Cruidites with assorted dips

Chocolate Brownies
Butterscotch Brownies

The brownies may be made a week ahead and frozen, or they may be made the day ahead of the party.

If you are serving shrimp it should be cooked, cleaned and refrigerated the day ahead. Serve with your favorite cocktail sauce.

The chicken wings may be prepared the day ahead, except for cooking. The dip for the vegetables may also be made a day or two in advance.

The day of the party: Pop the popcorn, slice the vegetables, prepare the potatoes, bake the wings and you're ready to cheer.

This menu adapts itself well to a buffet.

Parmesan Mustard Chicken Wings
Serves 4 – 6

1 cup butter melted
4 tablespoons Dijon-style mustard
¼ teaspoon ground (cayenne) red pepper
1 cup dry bread crumbs
1 cup grated Parmesan cheese
1 teaspoon ground cumin
½ teaspoon salt
Freshly ground pepper to taste
15 chicken wings (approximately), wing tip cut off and
        discarded. Cut or slice wings in half at joint

    Preheat oven to 450 degrees*. In a shallow dish, whisk together the melted butter, mustard and cayenne. In another dish combine the bread crumbs, Parmesan cheese, cumin, salt and pepper.

    Dip each wing piece into butter mixture then coat with crumb mixture.

    Arrange in a shallow baking pan. Bake for 20 minutes. Turn wings and continue baking an additional 20 minutes. Total baking time is approximately 40 minutes.

    Serve hot or at room temperature.

*The high baking temperature and the butter will cause the oven to smoke during cooking. However, the high temperature is necessary to ensure a golden brown wing. I usually cook the wings ahead of time and serve them at room temperature to avoid the smoke while I am entertaining.

Baked Potato Skins

Russet (baking) potatoes – allow one potato per person
Olive oil for brushing potato skins
Sweet paprika for sprinkling on the skins
Kosher salt for sprinkling on the skins
Sour cream as an accompaniment, if desired

Scrub potatoes, pat dry, rub with olive oil and wrap in aluminum foil. Bake in a 425 degree oven for about one hour or until a fork easily pierces through the potato. Let cool.

Halve potato lengthwise, and scoop out pulp, leaving ¼ inch shell. Cut each shell in half again, lengthwise, and arrange strips on a baking sheet. Reserve scooped-out potato for another use.

Brush strips with olive oil, sprinkle with paprika, salt and pepper. Potatoes may be made ahead up to this point. They may be kept at room temperature for an hour or two.

Bake in the middle of a preheated 425 degree oven for 20 to 25 minutes, or until crisp and golden brown. Serve with sour cream, garnished with fresh chives, if desired.

Change the Venue! It is amazing the difference it makes when you change the location of your meals. Have Sunday dinner in the dinning room instead of the kitchen. Watch the football game in the kids' playroom and have dinner there. Or try spreading a blanket on the backyard and dine alfresco.

An everyday meal becomes a special occasion. Everyone feels a little more festive – a little more willing to talk and enjoy the meal. It's a fun time and a good family get-together.

Types of Potatoes

Botanically, a potato is a swelling or tuber. It is part of the underground root of the potato plant, and is the site where energy is stored in the form of starch. At low temperatures (below 45 degrees F.) the starch converts to sugar and the potato blackens, which is why potatoes should not be stored in the refrigerator. <u>La Varenne Pratique</u> by Anne Willan

Russet – baking potato, often the skin is removed
    before eating. Peak season – summer and autumn

Idaho - a baking potato, considered the most popular in the United States. Peak season – summer and autumn

New – small, freshly dug potatoes which are still immature. Flavor is sweet and texture is waxy, best plainly boiled and usually served with skins left on. New potatoes are generally more expensive than other potatoes and very perishable. Peak season – spring

White Potato – another waxy potato, good for boiling and salads. Peak season – summer and autumn

Yukon Gold – a waxy potato with a sweet, buttery flavor. Peak season- summer

Sweet Potato – may be orange, white or yellow-fleshed. Has a sweet, chestnut flavor. Used for boiling, baking and pureeing. Peak season – autumn and winter

Yams – much larger than the sweet potato, but they may be used interchangeably. The flesh ranges from white to deep orange, red and even purple. They are less sweet, but more moist, than the sweet potato. Peak season – autumn and winter.

Brunswick Stew
Serves 6

Brunswick Stew is one of those wonderful, complete Southern dishes we discovered while living in the South. It has a little bit of everything, is nutritionally correct and contains the grace of good Southern food and hospitatlity. It is one of our favorite dishes to offer weary travelers their first night visiting us.

3 tablespoons olive oil
1 ½ pounds boneless, skinless chicken meat, cut into bite-size pieces.
¾ pound ground beef
1 medium onion, chopped
½ pound Polish Kielbasa sausage, cut into bite-size pieces
2½ cups chicken broth
1 28-ounce can tomatoes, chopped, with liquid
1 medium potato, peeled and chopped into ½ inch cubes
1 cup frozen lima beans
1 cup frozen corn kernels
½ cup frozen peas
1 teaspoon red pepper flakes
1 teaspoon salt
Freshly ground pepper to taste

In a large kettle (about 5 quarts), heat oil and sauté chicken pieces until brown. Remove chicken. In same kettle, sauté ground beef and onion until beef is brown. Drain any fat.

To the beef, add Polish Kielbasa, browned chicken, chicken broth, tomatoes, vegetables and spices. Bring mixture to a boil. Reduce heat to a simmer and continue to cook for approximately one hour. Adjust seasonings. May be made ahead and reheated. Also freezes well. All that is needed to complete the meal is some bread or biscuits.

Home from the Hospital

Whether for family or friend, there is nothing more healing than a home cooked meal after a stay in the hospital. This meal travels well. It may be frozen, in case there are numerous dinners made for the same night, and it is guaranteed to soothe the soul of a tired patient.

Chicken Pot Pie
Mixed Green Salad with Raspberry Dressing
Crusty Bread

Mint Chocolate Brownies

Chicken Pot Pie
Serves 4 – 6

I don't know why Chicken Pot Pie has such a bad rap. It is a delicious, good-for-you, soul warming meal.

Yet, it is often just served to young children and is usually purchased readymade, frozen.

Homemade Chicken Pot Pie is wonderful! It is as wonderful for adults as it is for children, and it is good enough for company.

It is also one of my favorite meals to take to friends in need – whether they have just had a new baby, been sick, or I simply need to let them know I care. It is especially suited for this purpose in that it is a meal in itself and freezes very well.

3 cups cooked chicken (meat from a 3 – 4 pound chicken),
    cut into bite-size pieces
1 tablespoon butter
1 tablespoon olive oil
⅓ cup celery, diced (about 1 stalk)
⅓ cup onion, diced
⅓ cup carrot, diced
⅓ cup red bell pepper, diced
3 tablespoons flour
2 cups chicken stock
⅓ cup milk or cream
2 tablespoons Madeira wine or sweet sherry
⅓ cup frozen peas
1 teaspoon salt
Freshly ground pepper to taste
1 pastry for a 2-crust 9-inch pie (p. 145)

Preheat oven to 425 degrees. Melt butter and olive oil in a large pan over medium heat. Add all vegetables except peas, and sauté until onions are translucent and other vegetables are soft, about 5 to 10 minutes.

Add the 3 tablespoons of flour and cook and stir for 1 minute – whisk in 2 cups chicken stock and increase heat to high and continue to whisk until thick Remove from heat.

Stir in cream, wine, chicken and peas. Add salt and pepper to taste.

Line a 9-inch pie pan with one crust. Pour in filling. Cover with top crust. Seal edges and flute. Cut slits in center to allow steam to escape. Cook in 425 degree oven until crust is brown and center begins to bubble, 30 – 35 minutes. The pot pie may be frozen before cooking or after cooking. If frozen before cooking, place frozen pie in oven and extend cooking time. If frozen after cooking, place frozen pie in preheated 350 degree oven and cook until warmed through – about 30 minutes.

Serve plain or accompanied with a fruit or green salad.

Too Busy To Cook?
Everyone says they're too busy to cook. Bologna! It's just a question of priority. One could easily be too busy to do laundry, too busy to watch TV, too busy to read, or too busy to exercise – and often we are.
But for some unknown reason, everyone is America seems to agree that they are all too busy to cook. I challenge you to change your priorities for one week. Make cooking a nutritious and delicious meal for yourself and your family, a daily top priority. Put this creation before all else – before the nightly news, before the housework, before the exercise class, before paying the bills. I think you will find a little time put into this meal will create a special magic in your family. This magic could be so strong that one might be convinced to make cooking a family meal a high priority in their life. Then neighbors might be convinced to cook family meals – and who knows – soon there might be books written and newspaper headlines on how Americans are too busy cooking to watch TV!!!

Presidents' Day Birthday Dinner

It was shortly after a February dinner party that my children asked why Daddy and I were the only ones who had dinner parties. Why couldn't they have a dinner party, they asked. Why not, I thought. So we decided to have a birthday dinner party for Presidents Washington and Lincoln.

The kids made the invitations. Everyone was allowed to invite one friend. The party was to be on Presidents' Day from 5:30 – 8 p.m. Each guest was asked to bring one interesting fact about either President.

We decorated the dinning room with pictures of Abe and George. For the centerpiece I put some white carnations in a bowl, added a few small American flags and the crowning touch was sparklers I had left over from the Fourth of July. My oldest son also made patriotic place cards for the occasion.

I was a little nervous about having all these children (ranging in age from 4 to 8) in my dinning room, but it was a great event. The facts kept all of us laughing and talking throughout the meal. At dessert we sang Happy Birthday to George and Abe and lit the sparklers, a grand finale.

For party favors, I gave each child a notepad with the 50 states on it and a patriotic pencil.

It was a great party and one the children have often asked me to repeat.

Presidents' Dinner
Presidential Punch (your favorite punch with
Maraschino cherries frozen in ice cubes)
Walnuts served in the shell with a nut cracker (George
used to break them open with his teeth)
Roasted Chicken
Sweet Potato and Apple Tart
Spinach Soufflé
Buttermilk Biscuits
Cherry Pie with whip cream or ice cream

Roast Chicken
Serves 4

There must be hundreds of methods to roasting a chicken. Each one claims to be "the best" and "the only way" to roast the fowl. If you have a method you like and it produces a tasty, moist bird – stick with it.

I have found this method of roasting the simplest, with the end result producing a moist and flavorful chicken with delicious drippings that can be served over the chicken or converted into a Fresh Herb Sauce.

One 3 – 4 pound chicken
Juice of 1 lemon
1 bunch of herbs (such as parsley, basil, thyme, rosemary, oregano – or any combination), optional
1-2 tablespoons olive oil
1 small onion, peeled and quartered
1-2 carrots, scrubbed and cut in half
1 stalk celery
½ cup dry white wine

To calculate roasting time for the bird, allow 15 – 20 minutes per pound. The bird will be done when a meat thermometer registers 175 – 180 degrees.

Add an additional 15 – 20 minutes "resting" time from completion of roasting until carving time.

The chicken should be at room temperature when you begin roasting. A cold chicken will not cook evenly.

The carrots, celery and onion are added to flavor the juices from the bird. These vegetables are called a mirepoix.

Preheat oven to 425 degrees. Rinse the bird well, inside and out, pat dry. Remove any of the visible yellow fat from inside or on the skin of the bird.

Sprinkle inside of chicken with salt and pepper and juice of ½ lemon. If using herbs, stuff them into the cavity.

Brush outside of chicken with olive oil and juice of remaining ½ lemon. Sprinkle outside with salt and pepper.

Place bird, breast side up, in a roasting pan- place in bottom ⅓ of oven. Roast for 15 minutes. Reduce heat to 350 degrees. Place carrots, celery and onion in bottom of pan. Pour wine over chicken.

Continue to roast, basting the bird with pan juices every 20 minutes, until done. Remove from roasting pan. Cover with foil and let stand 15 – 20 minutes before carving.

To reserve the drippings from the chicken, remove vegetables. Skim the fat from pan drippings. Place roasting pan with drippings over a medium heat and bring to a boil. Several additional tablespoons of white wine may be added at this point to help deglaze (scraping the brown particles from the bottom of) the pan. Continue to boil until mixture is reduced and slightly thickened. The drippings may now be spooned over the chicken when it is served, passed alongside, or converted into a Fresh Herb Sauce.

"Great cooking is the source of great happiness."
-   **Escoffier**

Fresh Herb Sauce
Serves 4 – 6

This sauce is wonderful over vegetables as well as poultry. Follow the directions for Roast Chicken. The sauce may be made with milk which will create a white sauce or a sauce béchamel. Or the sauce may be made with chicken stock which will create a sauce veloute. Both are equally delicious.

Drippings from Roast chicken
Milk or chicken stock
1 tablespoon butter
2 tablespoons flour
2 tablespoons fresh herbs (such as a combination of
    parsley, thyme, basil), chopped

Place drippings in a measuring cup. Add enough stock or milk to measure one cup. In a small saucepan, melt butter, add flour and cook and stir for 1 minute or until bubbling. Slowly whisk in milk or stock, stirring constantly.

Continue to cook and stir until mixture comes to a boil and becomes thick. Reduce heat and stir in herbs. Remove from heat, add salt and pepper to taste.

The designation of mother as a job description is unacceptable because " it fails to state principal professions, vocations or occupations" as required by the state elections code.
-Oliver Cox, California State Staff Counsel

This quote was found in the San Francisco Chronicle newspaper on February 10, 1997 in regards to Denise de Ville, who wished to be listed as "Mother" on the ballot in her race for County Board of Supervisors.

Cheese and Spinach Soufflé
4 – 6 servings

There are few dishes that create a more spectacular presentation than a soufflé. They are quite simple to make, and delicious to eat. This recipe is adapted from The Fannie Farmer Cookbook

This soufflé is a good accompaniment for chicken or fish. With a cup of cooked ham added to it, it is a meal in itself. It is also the only way my nine-year-old daughter will ever eat spinach.

If serving the soufflé for company prepare everything before the guests arrive – accept the egg whites. They must be beaten and folded into the soufflé immediately before baking.

Bring the soufflé to the table as soon as it is done, everyone should have the right to appreciate such beauty before it collapses. Yes, all soufflés will fall in slightly as they cool. There is nothing a cook can do.

1 bunch fresh spinach, cleaned, stems removed, steamed or boiled until cooked, squeezed dried and chopped – or one 10-ounce package frozen chopped spinach, cooked and squeezed dried.
¼ cup butter
¼ cup flour
1 cup milk
1 cup grated cheddar cheese (other cheeses may be substituted)
½ teaspoon salt
1/8 teaspoon ground (cayenne) red pepper
1/8 teaspoon nutmeg
Freshly grated pepper to taste
4 egg yolks beaten until light
4 egg whites
¼ cup freshly grated Parmesan cheese

Preheat oven to 325 degrees. Heat water which will be poured into a pan where the soufflé will bake.

In a saucepan melt the butter. Blend in the four and gradually whisk in milk, cook over medium heat, stirring constantly until thick and smooth.

Add spinach, cheddar cheese, salt, cayenne, nutmeg, and ground pepper. Stir and remove from heat. Stir in beaten egg yolks and set pan aside. (This mixture may sit at room temperature for an hour or so, if necessary)

Beat egg whites until stiff. Stir one tablespoon of the whites into the yolk mixture then fold in the rest.

Spoon mixture into an ungreased 1 quart soufflé dish. Top with Parmesan cheese. Set soufflé dish in a baking pan, add enough hot water to reach half way up the soufflé dish. Bake 30 to 45 minutes or until soufflé is firm and brown. Try not to open and close the oven door while the soufflé is baking. One peek after 30 minutes should be sufficient to let you know if the soufflé is done or if it needs a few more minutes.

Squeezed dried spinach – This is a great job for any youngster who happens to be hanging around the kitchen at this time. It is not my favorite job, but my second son just loves to squeeze that green stuff until every drop of water is gone.

Separating Eggs – Another great job for kids! They love it. I don't know why, they just do. However, I suggest you only teach this culinary technique on a day when you have lots of patience and plenty of extra eggs.

Macaroni and Cheese
Serves 4-6

There are few better comfort foods than macaroni and cheese. Unfortunately, there have been so many boxed or frozen varieties that people often forget how wonderful homemade macaroni and cheese truly is. Use your favorite cheese and your favorite type of pasta to make this dish personally special. The addition of cooked ham or turkey takes this recipe from a hearty side dish to a meal in itself.

My cousin, Barbara Smith of Bristol, Virginia, suggested the Worcestershire sauce. An excellent addition in that it cuts the richness of the cheese.

This recipe doubles well, may be made ahead, and also freezes well.

½ pound pasta, cooked and drained; macaroni, rotini, penne and even spaghetti broken into bite sized pieces work well
½ pound cheese, cut into chunks; Velveeta, Cheddar, American, and Gruyere all work well. Our family likes a combination of Velveeta and Cheddar.
½ cup milk
1 tablespoon butter
¼ teaspoon salt
Dash cayenne pepper
Dash Worcestershire sauce
2 cups cooked and chopped turkey or ham, optional
¼ cup dried bread crumbs

Cook and drain the pasta. Grease a 1½ quart casserole. Preheat oven to 350 degrees.

Place a double broiler over medium heat. In the top of the double broiler place cheese, milk, butter, and spices. Simmer and stir until all ingredients are melted and mixed. Toss cheese mixture with drained pasta. Add turkey or ham, if using. Place mixture in greased casserole dish. Top with bread crumbs. Casserole may be made and frozen at this point.

Bake macaroni and cheese for about 30 minutes or until bubbly.

"Never eat more than you can lift."
-Miss Piggy

Valentine's Day Dinner for Two

A simple Valentine's Day dinner at home with candlelight and soft music can create one of the most romantic evenings possible.

Ship the children to grandma and grandpa's for the evening or wait until the little darlings are in bed to share this delicious and lovely meal.

Begin the evening with a few reputed aphrodisiacs, then move on to the main course, followed by a heavenly chocolate dessert.

Champagne served with Oysters, Crayfish, or Caviar

Linguine with Red Clam Sauce
Mixed green salad with blue cheese, apples, and caramelized nuts
Bread

Red Chocolate Cake

The clam sauce may be made ahead of time as can the salad and the cake.

Be sure to serve a nice red wine with the linguine. The only last minute preparations should be assembling the salad, cooking the linguine, and reheating the sauce.

"Without bread, without wine, love is nothing."
-French Proverb

Linguine with Red Clam Sauce
Serves 2

A romantic and spicy dinner for two, although the recipe may be easily doubled or tripled.

1½ pounds live cherrystone clams
½ cup dry red wine
1½ teaspoon minced garlic
1 tablespoon olive oil
1 16-ounce can tomatoes, drained and chopped
½ teaspoon dried oregano
½ teaspoon dried thyme
½ teaspoon red pepper flakes
½ teaspoon fennel seeds
2 tablespoons minced fresh parsley
¼ pound dried linguine

Scrub clams well and soak them in cold water for several minutes to remove the sand inside the shells.

In a medium saucepan bring the wine to a boil, add the clams, cover and continue cooking for 5-7 minutes or until clams open. Discard any unopened clams. Transfer clams to a small bowl. Reserve the liquid from the pan in which the clams were cooked.

In a medium saucepan, heat the olive oil. Add garlic and sauté over medium-low heat, being careful not to brown the garlic. Strain the clam cooking liquid through a fine sieve lined with a dampened paper towel. This will remove any sand from the liquid. Pour the strained liquid into the sauté pan. Add tomatoes, oregano, thyme, red pepper flakes, fennel, and salt and pepper to taste. Bring to a boil. Reduce heat and simmer for approximately 20 minutes or until mixture thickens slightly. May be made ahead up to 24 hours ahead at this point. Keep refrigerated until ready to use.

In a large pot of boiling, salted water cook the linguine for 8-10 minutes, or until it is al dente, drain it well.

Add the clams and parsley to the red sauce and cook until heated through, about 5-10 minutes.

Place linguine in bowls and spoon clam sauce over top. Serve with freshly grated Parmesan cheese, if desired.

"If you live near the shore, gather your own clams if possible – a sport I loved to indulge in as a child."
- **James Beard, Theory & Practice of Good Cooking**

Mardi Gras

I can't believe I spent thirty-some years of my life eating pancakes on Shrove Tuesday or Fat Tuesday (the day before the beginning of Lent), when I could have been indulging in gumbo, jambalaya, etouffee, and the like.

I was thirty-nine years old on my first trip to New Orleans. It was January and the beginning of Mardi Gras season. All the houses had festive wreaths of green, gold, and purple (the colors of Mardi Gras). There was a feeling of party in the air, and the food was wonderful. Upon returning home I began planning our first Mardi Gras Party.

Mardi Gras is a wonderful excuse to party and eat well. It is often thought of as an adult party night, but it can be a fun family night as well.

For our first Mardi Gras party, we invited the grandparents. Everyone wore masks and festive clothes. The children entertained the adults with fortune telling, juggling, dancing, and mime, just as you would see on the streets of New Orleans.

The evening was highlighted by the eating of the King Cake and the crowning of the King for the night.

The King Cake, or the Twelfth Night Cake, is a big part of the Mardi Gras tradition. The large cake, shaped like a thick oval crown and decorated with candied fruit and colored sugar is prepared in New Orleans bakeries for the period between Twelfth Night (January 6th) and Ash Wednesday. A bean or a tiny china baby doll is baked into the cake and the person who gets the slice containing the bean or doll is king or queen for a week and must also provide a new King Cake to be served at the week's end. And so every week brings a new cake and a new king or queen. This ritual is a popular custom among family groups and in offices in New Orleans.

New Orleanians usually do not bake their own King Cakes. Since they are available freshly baked in a wide range of size and prices. But, if you know how to make a coffee cake, you should have no trouble following these general instructions for putting together a King Cake. The cake should be an oval ring about 2½ inches thick and 3 inches high. It is decorated with colored sugar and candied fruit and is supposed to look like a jeweled crown. A bean or a doll is baked into the batter or pushed into the finished cake from underneath- just so long as it is done secretly, so no one knows which slice will designate the monarch.

If you have a crown on hand that's great, otherwise have the children make a paper crown to be worn by the lucky person receiving the bean or doll.*

*Information provided by The New Orleans Cookbook by Rima and Richard Colin

Mardi Gras Dinner

Shrimp Remoulade

Green Gumbo
Chicken and Sausage Jambalaya *or* **Fried Catfish**
Bread or Muffins

King Cake

Chicken Sausage Jambalaya
Serves 4-6

1 pound boneless skinless chicken breasts
½ pound Polish Kielbasa, slice in ¼ inch rounds
2 tablespoons olive oil
1 medium onion, chopped
1 cup chopped celery
1 cup chopped green bell peppers
1 tablespoon minced garlic
3 cups chicken stock
1 28-ounce can of tomatoes, chopped with liquid
1½ cups long grain rice

Seasoning Mix
2 whole bay leaves
1 teaspoon ground (cayenne) red pepper
1 teaspoon ground black pepper
1½ teaspoon salt
1 teaspoon dried thyme leaves
¼ teaspoon rubbed sage

 Preheat oven to 350 degrees. In a large over-proof frying pan (12 inches), or a Dutch oven, heat olive oil. Sauté chicken breasts until brown. Remove and set aside with sliced Polish Kielbasa. In the same pan sauté onions, celery, bell pepper, and garlic until soft. Add chicken stock, chopped tomatoes and their liquid and bring to a boil. Add rice, stir and reduce to a simmer. Mix seasonings in a small bowl and add to mixture.
 Cut chicken into bite-size pieces. Add chicken and Polish Kielbasa to simmering mixture. Cover and bake in preheated oven for about 1 hour or until rice is tender. Stir occasionally. If more liquid is needed during baking, add additional chicken stock or water.

Fried Catfish
Serves 4-6

2 pounds catfish
1 cup buttermilk
1 cup flour
½ cup cornmeal
2 teaspoons Creole or Cajun Seasoning
Vegetable oil for frying

Place catfish fillets in a medium dish with buttermilk and let soak at least one hour and up to 24 hours in the refrigerator.

Combine flour, cornmeal, and seasoning on wax paper. Drain fish and sprinkle with salt and pepper. Dip each fish into flour mixture and coat both sides.

In a large skillet place about a ¼ inch of vegetable oil and heat to 360 degrees. Working in batches, cook each fillet in oil until crispy brown, turn and cook the other side. Remove fish to an oven-proof pan. Place pan with fish in 250 degree oven. Continue cooking until all fillets are done. Fish may sit in 250 degree oven up to one hour before serving.

Winter III

Desserts

Buche de Noel
Yule Log
Serves 10

Buche de Noel is a traditional French Christmas Dessert. This flourless chocolate cake rolled into the shape of a log has recently become a classic holiday dessert in America as well. A rich chocolate cake with whipped cream filling and meringue butter cream icing is a dessert "to die for". Eating the cake, however, is only half the fun. Decorating the log with bits of holly, sugared cranberries, ivy, or other greenery brings out the creativity in all of us. It is great fun making a cake look like a log: it's easy and brings a lot of pleasure and a little bit of amusement to the holiday season.

For the Cake:
6 eggs, separated, at room temperature
¾ cup sugar, divided
⅓ cup cocoa
1½ teaspoons vanilla
Dash of salt
½ cup powered sugar

For the Filling:
1½ cup whipping cream
½ cup confectioners' sugar
¼ cup cocoa
2 teaspoons Kahlua Liqueur*
1 teaspoon vanilla

For Meringue Butter Cream Icing:
3 egg whites
Dash of salt
¼ teaspoon cream of tartar
1⅓ cups sugar
⅓ cup water

2 cups semi-sweet chocolate chips
3 tablespoons Kahlua Liqueur
1 tablespoon vanilla
½ pound unsalted butter, softened

To make the Cake:

Preheat oven to 375 degrees. Grease a 15" x 10" jelly roll pan and line it with wax paper. Grease again. In a large bowl, beat egg whites at high speed until soft peaks form. Add ¼ cup sugar, 2 tablespoons at a time, beating until stiff peaks form.

In a separate bowl, beat yolks at high speed, adding remaining ½ cup sugar, 2 tablespoons at a time. Beat several minutes until mixture turns a pale yellow, forms ribbons, and is very thick. Reduce speed to low, mix in cocoa, vanilla, and salt.

Gently fold chocolate mixture into egg whites. Spread evenly in pan and bake for 15 minutes or until surface springs back when gently pressed. Sift ½ cup confectioners' sugar in a 10" by 15" rectangle on a linen towel. Invert pan over sugar, lift off pan, peel off wax paper. Roll up cake, using towel as an aid. Place seam side down on a rack. Cool 30 minutes.

To make the Filling:

In a medium bowl combine all filling ingredients. Beat until thick. Refrigerate. Unroll cake and spread with filling. Roll again placing seam side down on a serving plate.

To make the Icing:

At medium speed beat egg whites until foamy. Add salt and cream of tartar. Beat on high until stiff peaks form.

In a saucepan combine sugar and water. Over high heat swirl, do not stir with a spoon, until sugar is dissolved and liquid is clear. Bring to a boil and continue to boil until mixture reaches 238 degrees on a candy thermometer. On low speed, <u>very</u> slowly, beat sugar mixture into egg whites.

Beat on high speed for several minutes, or until mixture is cool.

Melt chocolate with Kahlua and vanilla. Add to meringue mixture. Gradually beat in butter. Chill until it reaches a spreading consistency.

Frost cake with meringue butter cream. Cut a 1-2 inch diagonal slice from end of cake. Glue this piece on top of cake with icing to simulate a "bump" on the log. Run a fork along the length of cake to make "bark" designs. Decorate with holly, sugared cranberries, or other greens.

May be frozen.

*Substitute your favorite liqueur for Kahlua in both filling and icing (Try Amaretto or Chambord)

Sugared Cranberries:

Roll fresh cranberries in lightly beaten egg whites and then in granulated sugar.

***any left over icing is delicious if melted and put on top of ice cream. The icing will keep for several days in the refrigerator.

Red Chocolate Cake
For
Christmas or Valentine's
Serves 8-10

     The story goes that when Grandma visited New York in 1959 she had this cake at the Waldorf-Astoria Hotel. It was so delicious she requested, and received, the recipe. Our family has been serving it at Christmas ever since. My children love this cake so much that we decided to change the icing from green to pink and serve this dessert at Valentine's Day as well as Christmas day.

     Whether iced with green, pink, or white, this cake is a treat for all chocolate lovers.

For the Cake:
½ cup butter
1½ cups sugar
2 eggs
2 ounces red food coloring
2 tablespoons unsweetened cocoa
1 cup buttermilk
2 ¼ cups flour
1 teaspoon salt
1 teaspoon vanilla
1 teaspoon baking soda
1 tablespoon apple cider vinegar

For the Icing:
1 cup milk
5 tablespoons flour
1 cup sugar
1 cup butter (2 sticks), softened
1 teaspoon vanilla
Several drops green food coloring (or whatever color you choose to ice the cake)

To make the Cake:

Preheat oven to 350 degrees. Butter and flour two 8-inch cake pans.

Cream butter and sugar until light and fluffy. Beat in eggs. Make a paste of the food coloring and cocoa. Stir into egg mixture. Add buttermilk and combine.

Sift flour and salt. Stir into buttermilk/egg batter. Stir in vanilla. Dissolve baking soda in vinegar. Blend into batter, beating as little as possible.

Divide between cake pans. Bake 30 minutes or until done. Cool cakes on rack before removing from pan.

To make the Icing:

In a small saucepan over medium heat combine the flour and milk. Stir until thick and difficult to stir. Cool in refrigerator. Cream butter and sugar until light and fluffy. Stir in vanilla. When flour and milk has cooled, beat in butter and sugar mixture. Stir in drops of food color until desired color is reached.

To ice the Cake:

To make a 3 layer cake: Divide one cake in half, length-wise with a serrated knife. Place one half layer on cake plate, ice. Top with second half layer, ice. Top with remaining cake, ice top and sides. Keep cake refrigerated until ready to serve.

To make four layers: Divide each cake in half, making four layers. Ice as above.

Soon her eye fell on a little glass box that was lying under the table: she opened it, and found in it a very small cake, on which the words "eat me" were beautifully marked in currants. "Well, I'll eat it," said Alice, "and if it makes me grow larger, I can reach the key: and if it makes me grow smaller, I can creep under the door: so either way I'll get into the garden, and I don't care what happen!"

She ate a little bit, and said anxiously to herself, "Which way? Which way?", holding her hand on the top of her head to see which way it was growing: and she was quite surprised to find that she remained the same size. To be sure, this is what generally happens when one eats cake: but Alice had to so much into the way of expecting nothing but out-of-the-way things to happen, that it seemed quite dull and stupid for life to go on in the common way.

So she set to work and very soon finished off the cake.

- <u>Alice's Adventures in Wonderland</u> by Lewis Carroll

Chocolate Mousse and Raspberry Cream Dacquoise
Serves 16

This is a show stopper dessert. Although the directions appear lengthy, they are simple to follow and the cake is easy to make. This recipe is adapted from Gourmet Magazine, January 1991.

"A dacquoise is a traditional cake of southwestern France. It consists of two or three layers of meringue, mixed with almonds or hazelnuts. The layers are sandwiched together with whipped cream or French butter cream, variously flavored."- **Larousse Gastronomique.**

For the meringues:
1 cup toasted almonds
2 cups sugar
½ teaspoon salt
1 cup egg whites (about 8 large eggs)
3 ounces bittersweet chocolate, melted

For the mousse:
7 ounces bittersweet chocolate, chopped
2 ounces unsweetened chocolate, chopped
3 tablespoons raspberry liqueur
⅓ cup strong brewed coffee
1 ¼ cups sugar
4 large egg whites
¼ teaspoon cream of tartar

For the whipped cream:
1 envelope (1 tablespoon) plus 2 teaspoons unflavored
    gelatin
¼ cup raspberry liqueur
4 cups heavy cream
¼ cup sugar
1 ½ teaspoons vanilla

For garnish:
3 ounces bittersweet chocolate, melted
About 1 cup frozen raspberries

Make the meringues: Line 3 baking sheets with parchment or foil and trace a circle, 11 inches in diameter on each sheet of parchment. Preheat oven to 250 degrees. In a food processor, grind the almonds with ½ cup of sugar, transfer the mixture to a bowl, and stir in ½ cup of remaining sugar and the salt, stirring until mixture is well combined.

In a large bowl with an electric mixer beat the egg whites with a pinch of salt until they hold soft peaks. Add remaining 1 cup sugar gradually beating. Continue to beat egg whites until they hold stiff glossy peaks. Fold in nut mixture.

Cover each 11 inch circle with ⅓ of the meringue nut mixture.

Bake the meringues on 3 evenly spaced racks or in batches of a preheated 250 degree oven, rotating the meringues from 1 rack to another every 20 minutes for 1 hour, or until they are firm when touched. Remove the parchment with meringues from the baking sheets, let the meringues cool and then peel off parchment, carefully. (The meringues may be made 3 days in advance when kept wrapped in plastic wrap, or freeze several weeks in advance.)

Trim the meringues to a uniform size, if necessary, with a serrated knife. Reserve the best looking meringue for the top layer. Spread the underside of 1 of the remaining meringues with the melted chocolate (this will be the middle layer), reserve it, chocolate side up, and put remaining meringue (this will be the bottom layer) on a large flat cake platter.

Make the mousse: In a bowl set over barely simmering water, melt the chocolate with the raspberry liqueur and coffee, whisking until the mixture is smooth, then remove from heat. In a small heavy saucepan, combine the sugar with ½ cup water and bring the mixture to a boil, stirring until the sugar is dissolved. Boil the syrup, undisturbed, until is registers 248 degrees on a candy thermometer. Remove the pan from heat.

In a large bowl, beat the egg whites with a pinch of salt until they are foamy, add the cream of tartar, and beat the egg whites until they hold soft peaks. With the mixer running, add the hot syrup in a stream to the stiff egg whites and beat the mixture on medium speed for 10 minutes or until it is cool. Whisk about 1 cup of the egg white mixture until the chocolate mixture to lighten it and then fold the chocolate mixture into the beaten egg whites.

Mound the mousse in the middle of the bottom meringue layer, top it with the chocolate-covered meringue layer, chocolate side up, and press the layer down gently until the mousse almost reaches the edge. Chill the cake for 1 hour, or until the mousse is set.

Make the whipped cream: In a very small saucepan, sprinkle the gelatin over the raspberry liqueur and 2 tablespoons water. Let it soften for 5 minutes. Heat mixture over low heat, stirring until the gelatin is dissolved. Let the gelatin cool as much as possible, while still remaining liquid. In a chilled large bowl beat the cream with sugar and the vanilla until it is thick and the beaters just begin to leave a mark. Add the gelatin mixture in a stream, beating – beat the mixture until it just holds stiff peaks. (Be careful not to over beat.)

Reserve ¼ of the whipped cream in a small bowl. Spread half of the remaining whipped cream on top of the chocolate covered meringue layer. Put the reserved top meringue on the whipped cream, pressing down gently. Spread the remaining whipped cream on the sides of the cake. Put the reserved whipped cream in a pastry bag fitted with a star tip and pipe it decoratively on the top and bottom edges of the cake.

Garnish the cake: Put the melted chocolate in small pastry bag fitted with a plain writing tip and pipe it in a spoke pattern on the top of the cake. Arrange the raspberries around the edge of the cake and make a circle of them in the center.

Chill the cake for at least 4 hours and up to 8 hours.

Use a serrated knife to cut the cake.

Cookies

Cookies are some of Americans most favorite desserts. Homemade cookies are always appreciated. However, no more so than at Christmas time. A tray, piled high with freshly baked cookies, will put a smile the face of any Scrooge.

Remember that most cookies freeze well, and also that the dough is often better if made a day in advance and kept refrigerated until baking time.

We have included our favorite cookie recipes here. They are all delicious any time of the year.

Chocolate Chip Cookies
Makes 4 – 5 dozen cookies

It is not necessary to have a bag of chocolate chips in order to make chocolate chip cookies. In fact, using a chocolate candy bar makes delicious, extra sweet cookies – or try using really fine quality chocolate or an extra special treat. There is nothing better than cookies make with hand chopped chocolate. Biting into a cookie with an extra large chip is like finding a little bit of heaven.

Of course, a bag of chocolate chips may be used instead of making your own chips, but I don't think it will taste quite as good.

12 ounces semisweet chocolate, broken into chips
½ pound butter (2 sticks), softened
¾ cup brown sugar
¾ cup sugar
2 eggs
1 teaspoon vanilla extract
2 cups flour
1 teaspoon baking powder
½ teaspoon salt

Preheat oven to 325 degrees. Cream butter with sugars until light and fluffy. Add eggs and vanilla, mix well.

Sift flour, soda, and salt together in a mixing bowl. Stir into butter-egg mixture. Add chocolate chips and mix. For variation: add 1 cup raisins or nuts.

Drop dough in teaspoon-size portions onto cookie sheet. Bake 8 – 10 minutes or until cookies begin to brown. Cool on wax paper.

The chocolate chip cookie is Americans overwhelmingly favorite cookie.
- Bon Appetit Magazine, January 1998

Oatmeal-Raisin-Bran Cookies
Makes about 5 dozen cookies

This cookie recipe came about by accident. While baking traditional oatmeal cookies one day, I realized I was short on flour. Searching for a substitution, I tried making up the difference with oat bran. The result was a more delicious, better texture cookie. Plus, it's better for you.

1 cup (2 sticks) butter, room temperature
1¼ cups packed brown sugar
½ cup sugar
2 large eggs
2 teaspoons vanilla extract
1½ cups flour
1 teaspoon baking soda
½ teaspoon salt
12 ounces semi-sweet chocolate chips (2 cups)
2 cups old fashioned oats
1 cup raisins
½ cup oat bran

Preheat oven to 375 degrees. In a large bowl, beat butter and sugars until smooth and creamy. Add eggs and vanilla and beat until blended. Sift flour, baking soda and salt into a medium bowl; stir into butter mixture. Add chocolate chips, oats, raisins and oat bran. Stir until well blended.

Drop dough by tablespoons onto an cookie sheet. Bake cookies until golden brown, but soft to the touch, about 12 minutes. Cool on wax paper.

Snickerdoodles
Makes 3 – 4 dozen cookies

I love the name of these cinnamon-sugar cookies, but unfortunately I don't know where it came from or why it is – but none the less – the cookies are simple to make, delicious, and particularly good with a cup of coffee in the morning. This is Lee Bailey's recipe.

1½ cups sugar
1 cup butter (2 sticks), softened
2 eggs
2¾ cups flour
2 teaspoons cream of tartar
1 teaspoon baking soda
¼ teaspoon salt
Topping:
¼ cup sugar
1 tablespoon cinnamon

In a large mixing bowl cream together the sugar and butter. Beat until light and fluffy. Add eggs, one at a time, beating well after each addition.

Sift together the flour, cream of tartar, baking soda and salt. Add the flour mixture in 4 parts to the sugar/egg batter – beat well after each addition.

Wrap dough in plastic wrap and refrigerate at least one hour. Dough may be made a day in advance.

Preheat oven to 400 degrees. In a small bowl, combine the sugar and cinnamon for topping. Roll dough into walnut-sized balls and roll balls in topping mixture. Place on cookie sheet, about 2 inches apart. Bake 8 – 10 minutes or until golden brown.

Snicker, vi.. to laugh in a half-suppressed manner
Doodle, v. to draw or to scribble
- **Random House Dictionary**
Snickerdoodle, ??????????

Rocks
Makes 8 – 9 dozen cookies

Grandma Michels' recipe, these cookies taste and smell of Christmas. Although their name and their appearance is not the most attractive – these bumpy little cookies are a favorite among the family and are included in every tray full of holiday goodies we make.

1½ cups sugar
1 cup butter
3 eggs
2½ cups flour
1½ teaspoons ground cloves
1 teaspoon cinnamon
1 teaspoon baking soda, dissolved in ¼ cup water
1 pound chopped dates
1 pound chopped walnuts
1 pound raisins (golden or black)

Preheat oven to 350 degrees. In a medium mixing bowl, cream together sugar and butter until light and fluffy. Beat in eggs, one at a time, beating well after each addition.

Sift together flour, cloves and cinnamon. Stir flour mixture into butter, egg mixture. Combine well. Add baking soda and water, dates, walnuts, and raisins.

Drop by teaspoons onto cookie sheet. Bake approximately 10 minutes or until bottoms begin to brown. Remove from cookie sheet and cool on wax paper.

Ever wonder what is Santa's favorite cookie?

Peppermint Candy Canes
Makes about 2 dozen cookies

 These pretty candy canes are a colorful addition to any holiday cookie tray. Adapted from Martha Stewart, these cookies have become a traditional part of our Christmas cookie repertoire.

1 pound butter (4 sticks)
2 cups sifted powdered sugar
2 eggs
1 teaspoon vanilla extract
1 teaspoon peppermint extract
¼ teaspoon salt
5 cups flour
¼ - ½ teaspoon red food coloring

Cream butter with powdered sugar until fluffy. Beat in eggs, vanilla, peppermint and salt. Sift flour and stir into butter/sugar mixture until blended.

Divide dough in half. Stir enough food coloring into one-half dough to color it evenly. Wrap both pieces of dough in wax paper or plastic wrap and refrigerate several hours or overnight.

Preheat oven to 350 degrees. Shape a teaspoon of plain dough (about the size of a nickel) into a 4-inch long cylinder. Do the same with a piece of the red dough. Twist the cylinders together and bend into a cane shape. Repeat with the rest of dough.

Place candy canes on a cookie sheet and bake for 8 – 10 minutes or until bottoms just begin to brown. Cool on wax paper. These cookies freeze well.

Christmas Sugar Cookies
Makes about 4 dozen cookies

Here are a few tips to help the cut-out sugar cookies hold shape during baking: Use cold, unsalted butter. Roll out a small amount of dough at a time – keeping the remaining dough refrigerated. Let baking sheets cool before reusing them (we stick ours in the freezer in-between batches).

These cookies are good plain or sprinkled with colored sugar before baking. However, they are best when baked, then iced with butter cream frosting and decorated with colored sugar and cinnamon drops.

1 cup butter (2 sticks)
1 cup sugar
2 eggs
½ teaspoon vanilla
½ teaspoon lemon juice
2¼ cups flour
1 teaspoon cream of tartar
½ teaspoon baking soda
¼ teaspoon salt
Cookie cutters

In a medium mixing bowl, cream together butter and sugar. Beat in eggs, then vanilla and lemon juice. In a small bowl sift together flour, cream of tartar, baking soda and salt. Stir into butter/sugar mixture. Wrap in wax paper or plastic wrap and refrigerate several hours or overnight.

Preheat oven to 350 degrees. On a lightly-floured surface roll dough to about 1/8 inch thick and cut out cookies with cookie cutters. Place cookies on a baking sheet. Bake 8 – 10 minutes or until edges begin to brown. Cool on wax paper. Let cool completely before icing.

Butter Cream Frosting

Makes enough frosting to ice one batch of sugar cookies
or
One 2-layer cake

1 pound confectioners' sugar
¼ pound butter (1 stick), room temperature
1 teaspoon vanilla extract
3 – 4 tablespoons milk

Cream sugar and butter together until light and fluffy. Beat in milk, one tablespoon at a time, until frosting is of a spreading consistency.

To ice cookies: Divide frosting into as many bowls as colors are desired. Place several drops of food color into frosting and stir until well mixed.

Ice cookies then decorate with colored sugars, sprinkles, cinnamon drops, chocolate chips and raisins.

Aniseed Cookies
Makes about 2 dozen cookies

Aniseed Cookies are a traditional Christmas cookie in New Mexico. We think they are an excellent dessert for a Cinco De Mayo celebration. This recipe is adapted from The Feast of Santa Fe by Huntley Dent.

½ cup butter (1 stick)
2/3 cup sugar
1 egg
1 teaspoon aniseed
1 tablespoon brandy
1½ cups flour
1 teaspoon baking powder
¼ teaspoon salt
¼ cup sugar, mixed with ½ teaspoon cinnamon for
    dredging.

Preheat oven to 350 degrees. In a medium mixing bowl cream together the butter and sugar until light and fluffy. Beat in eggs, aniseed and brandy.

In another bowl, sift together flour, baking powder and salt. Combine flour mixture with butter/sugar mixture until well blended.

Break off a piece of dough the size of a nickel and roll it into a ball. Dredge the ball in the sugar/cinnamon mixture. Place on a cookie sheet. Repeat until all the dough is used.

Cookies may be kept in a ball for a soft cookie or flattened with a fork for a crisp cookie.

Bake 8 – 10 minutes for until cookie begins to brown. Cool on wax paper.

Buckeyes
Makes about 5 dozen candies

These peanut butter – chocolate candies taste like Reece's Peanut Butter Cups – only better. They are a favorite of adults as well as children. This recipe is adapted from my sister-in-law Mary Scovanner.

1½ pounds powdered sugar
½ pound butter (2 sticks)
1 pound smooth peanut butter
12 ounces semi-sweet chocolate chips
¼ slab of paraffin
store-bought tube icing, optional

In a large mixing bowl, beat sugar, butter and peanut butter together until smooth. Using your hands, shape the dough into small balls, about the size of quarters. Chill the balls in the refrigerator for several hours or overnight.

Melt chocolate chips and paraffin in the top of a double boiler pan. Remove from heat. Using a toothpick, dip each ball into the chocolate. Place ball on wax paper until chocolate hardens. Use store-bought tube icing to cover the hole in the candy. During the holidays we use red and green icing to cover the holes.

These candies freeze very well and keep for a long time.

Paraffin Wax is usually found in the baking section of a grocery store, next to the canning items. It is used for coating fruit and vegetables and for glazing the crust of cheeses. It is used to help harden chocolate in candies and also for sealing jars of jam.

Mint Chocolate Brownies*

Makes 15 large servings

1/2 pound butter (2 sticks), room temperature
2 cups sugar
4 eggs
1 teaspoon vanilla extract
1 teaspoon peppermint extract
4 ounces unsweetened chocolate
1 ⅓ cups flour
2 teaspoons baking powder
Pinch salt
1 cup chopped nuts

Preheat oven to 325 degrees. Grease a 9x13 inch baking pan. In a mixing bowl, cream together butter and sugar until light and fluffy. Add eggs, one at a time, beating after each addition. Stir in vanilla and peppermint extract.

In the top of a double boiler or microwave, melt the chocolate. Stir melted chocolate into butter/sugar mixture.

In a medium bowl, sift together flour, baking powder and salt. Stir butter/sugar mixture into flour. Mix to combine. Stir in nuts.

Pour into prepared baking pan. Bake 40 minutes or until a cake tester placed in center of brownies comes out clean. Try not to over bake.

Cool on rack. Dust with powdered sugar, if desired. When cooled, cut into squares.

*If plain chocolate brownies are desired, use 2 teaspoons vanilla extract in place of the 1 teaspoon vanilla and 1 teaspoon peppermint.

Lemon Chess Pie
Serves 6

For years I was mystified by the name Chess Pie. Was it a pie to be eaten while playing chess? Or was there some sort of design you were to put on top of the pie to make it look like a chess board?

Chess Pie, however, has nothing to do with the game of Chess, I learned. It is simply a Southern pie made of eggs and milk – 'jess pie – as a Southerner might say. Thus 'jess pie became Chess Pie, a general description that can be applied to a wide variety of pies.

My Chess Pie is one of our favorite winter desserts. Use the California Meyer lemon, if possible, it is slightly less acidic than the regular lemon.

Pastry for 1, 9-inch pie crust (p.145)
¼ cup butter, room temperature
1 cup sugar
3 eggs
¼ cup buttermilk
1 teaspoon lemon zest
¼ cup lemon juice (juice of 2 -3 lemons)
Dash salt
Powdered sugar, optional

Preheat oven to 425 degrees. Line pie pan with crust and flute edges. Refrigerate until ready to fill.

In a medium mixing bowl, cream together the butter and sugar. Beat in eggs, one at a time. Mix in buttermilk, lemon zest, lemon juice and salt. Pour into pie crust.

Bake at 425 degrees for 15 minutes. Reduce heat to 350 degrees and continue to bake for an additional 20 minutes or until pie is set. Cool on rack. Dust with powdered sugar, if desired. Pie may be served at room temperature or cold.

Cherry Pie
Serves 6

We like to make cherry pie in the wintertime to celebrate George Washington's birthday. Consequently, we make our pie with canned cherries, rather than fresh.

2 16-ounce cans of red tart pitted cherries, in water,
    drained, juice reserved
1½ cups sugar, divided
4 tablespoons cornstarch
¼ teaspoon almond extract
1 tablespoon butter
Pastry for 2, 9-inch pie crusts(p.145)

Preheat oven to 400 degrees. Drain cherries, reserving ¾ cup of juice. In a medium saucepan combine ¾ cup sugar with cornstarch. Whisk in the ¾ cup of cherry juice. Cook and stir over medium heat until very thick. Remove from heat and stir in remaining ¾ cup sugar. Stir in drained cherries and almond extract.

Line pie pan with one pastry crust. Fill with cherry mixture. Dot with butter. Place on top crust. Seal and crimp edges. Cut slits in top crust to vent steam. Bake 50 – 60 minutes or until crust browns and filling begins to bubble. Cool pie on rack before serving.

Serve plain or with whipped cream or ice cream.

King Cake
Serves 10

Our King Cake is basically a sour cream coffee cake, cooked in a bundt pan and then decorated to resemble a crown. Leftovers are wonderful the next morning for breakfast. You may decorate the cake with colored icing (I like butter cream frosting) or colored sugar, as suggested. Just remember the colors of Mardi Gras are gold, purple and green.

½ pound butter (2 sticks)
2 cups sugar
2 eggs
1 cup sour cream
1 tablespoon vanilla extract
2 cups flour
1 tablespoon baking powder
¼ teaspoon salt
Tiny china doll or bean
Colored sugar for decorating
Candied fruit, optional

Preheatt oven to 350 degrees. Grease a 10-inch bundt pan and lightly dust inside with flour. Cream the butter and sugar until light and fluffy. Add eggs, one at a time, beating well after each addition. Add sour cream and vanilla, blending well.

In a separate bowl, sift together the flour, baking soda and salt. Fold dry ingredients into creamed mixture. Stir to blend, but do not over beat.

Pour batter into bundt pan. Drop bean or doll into batter. If cake is to be iced with frosting then bake as is. If using colored sugar, sprinkle over cake at this point. Bake for about 60 minutes for until a cake tester inserted into center comes out clean.

After cake has cooled, it may be turned out on a plate and iced. Candied fruit may then be applied to icing to resemble crown jewels.

Remember, whoever receives the bean or doll in his or her slice of the cake is named King.!!!

Index

A

B

Frosting, Butter Cream, 307

K

L

M

Q

R

Rainbow Trout, Grilled, 38
Raspberry Salad Dressing, 85
Red Chocolate Cake, 293
Ribs on the Barbie, 103
Rice:
    Risotto with Herbs de Provence, 44
    Spanish Rice, 56
Rhubarb-Strawberry Ice cream, 62
Rhubarb-Strawberry Pie, 66
Rocks, Cookies, 304

S

Salad:
    Blue Cheese Salad Dressing, 84
    Caesar Salad Sans Egg, 155
    Caesar Salad, Traditional, 154
    Chicken Salad, 35
    Fillet of Beef Salad, 124
    Grilled Chicken Nicoise, 126
    Mixed green with Blue Cheese, Apple and
        Caramelized Nut, 229
    Poppy Seed Salad Dressing, 22
    Raspberry Salad Dressing, 85
    Red Potato Salad with Dill, 120
    Two Bean Salad, 121
    Versatile Salad Dressing, 230
Salsa, Hot Summer, 78
Salsa, Strawberry and Mango, 96
Salmon Cakes, 216
Salmon, Cold Glazed, 211
Sauces:
    Fresh Herb Sauce, 277
    Georgia Bar-B-Que, 101
    Hollandaise, 8

T

V

W

Y

Z

Zucchini:
    Bread, 86
    Cream Soup, 81
    Single Layer Chocolate Cake, 130

Made in the USA